Edible Gardens

Elizabeth Peters
Editor

BROOKLYN
BOTANIC
GARDEN

Elizabeth Peters
DIRECTOR OF
PUBLICATIONS

Meredith Ford
ASSOCIATE EDITOR

Dr. Mark Tebbitt
SCIENCE EDITOR

Joni Blackburn
COPY EDITOR

Elizabeth Ennis
ART DIRECTOR

Scot Medbury
PRESIDENT

Elizabeth Scholtz
DIRECTOR
EMERITUS

Handbook #196

Copyright © 2011 by Brooklyn Botanic Garden, Inc.

ISBN 978-1-889538-75-4

Printed in China by Ocean Graphics Press.

♻ Printed with soy-based inks on
postconsumer recycled paper.

Guides for a Greener Planet are published by
Brooklyn Botanic Garden, 1000 Washington Avenue,
Brooklyn, NY 11225.

Learn more at bbg.org/handbooks.

Cover: Many food plants have not only culinary but also decorative virtues, like this purple-hued kale (*Brassica oleracea* var. *sabellica* 'Osaka Red'). Above: Design elements such as color, texture, and form can be employed to great effect in the vegetable garden.

Edible Gardens

The Magic of Food Plants ELIZABETH PETERS 4

Beauty and Bounty in the Garden BARBARA DAMROSCH 8

Edible Garden Designs 16

A Delicious Front Yard MEGHAN RAY 18

An Ornamental Potager CAYLEB LONG 22

A Native Food Forest and Meadow ULRICH LORIMER 26

A Home Orchard JOAN MCDONALD 30

Container Gardens JENNIFER WILLIAMS 34

A Public Garden CALEB LEECH 42

A Children's Garden ASHLEY GAMELL 46

Encyclopedia of Edible Garden Plants JONI BLACKBURN 50

Edible Garden Plants at a Glance 108

Planning Your Edible Garden 111

For More Information 112

Contributors 114

Index 116

The Magic of Food Plants

Elizabeth Peters

Plants do something magical, something that forms the basis of life on our planet. When sunlight falls on them, plants use chlorophyll to trap some of the sun's energy in the molecules that they assemble using water and carbon dioxide in the process called photosynthesis. (Most plants do this. Some are parasitic, relying on other plants' work to survive.) Once this energy is captured, swept out of thin air and packed into new molecules called sugars, it is available to support the plant's growth and reproduction.

Plants distribute these sugars throughout their bodies to store them near all the cells that need energy for metabolism. Some sugars are converted into more complex molecules, including amino acids and the long cellulose molecules that form a plant's structure. Many are used to make the plant's flowers, fruit, and seeds. And because the plant cannot control its environment, it stores excess sugars against a future time of need—literally saving for a cloudy day (or, more often, a dry one).

Animals, including us humans, can't harvest energy directly from the sun in this manner. To get the energy we need to live, we eat plants (or animals that ate plants) and tap into the energy that was originally embodied in those sugars. In this way, we rely on plants for our own growth, movement, thinking—for our very existence. Life is solar powered.

Cultivating Plants as Food

Long ago, humans discovered some food plants to be more useful than others. We learned to avoid those that made us sick or were too tough to digest and instead sought out those with the greatest rewards: sweet, sugary fruits; starchy roots full of stored sugars; fat- and protein-rich seeds. At first we foraged for what nature offered us, migrating to follow what was seasonally available. At some point, probably over 10,000 years ago, humans began to tame and cultivate plants, and the art of agriculture began.

The earliest domesticated food plants were probably chosen for practical traits like easily collectible and storable seeds, speed of germination, and reliability of growth. Other desirable traits would have included a quick progression from seed to harvest, a bountiful reward of edible parts, and crops that could be collected over time or that would store well. These traits were favored as seeds from the most successful plants were collected and replanted over generations. Over time, this has led to forms of cultivated plants that are very different from their wild cousins.

Look through a kitchen garden seed catalog, and you will see a carnival of plants with edible parts exaggerated to the point of caricature. Carrots hoard sugars in a gigantic taproot; corn offers up an obscenely large seed head; lettuces produce a

Food plants like this leafy chard (*Beta vulgaris* var. *cicla*) as well as ornamentals like the roses above trap energy from the sun in the sugars that they (and we) require to live.

bounty of sweet leaves on the shortest stem you can imagine. Nowadays, in addition to practical considerations, we cultivate food plants for entertainment, selecting for features like taste, color, and form.

And we cultivate them for their stories. Foods embody memories, both our own personal memories (Grandma's rhubarb pie) and our cultural memories (okra came to the South with the African slave trade). Seeing these familiar foods in an unfamiliar setting—not the grocery aisle but the garden bed—provides a great jumping-off point for talking about nature, nutrition, economics, seasonality, and more.

Edible Plants at Brooklyn Botanic Garden

With this in mind, BBG's Herb Garden was expanded and redesigned in 2010 to offer a dynamic educational space for classes and visitors alike. Dedicated to plants grown for human use, the garden is designed to be a decorative potager, or kitchen garden, that freely mixes medicinal and culinary herbs, vegetables, berries, fruit trees, and flowers that reflect the diverse cultures and culinary traditions of Brooklyn's neighborhoods. A central bed of annual vegetables changes with the seasons, while a small orchard and fences of espaliered and trained trees and shrubs show the production of fruit over time.

Another garden dedicated to edible plants is BBG's Children's Garden, where children have been growing flowers, vegetables, and herbs since 1914. Each year, over 800 children nurture and harvest their own food plants in victory garden–style plots. In the process they learn about botany, plant families, seed germination, and the seasonal cycles of nature.

Edible plants flourish in many other gardens at BBG, including the Native Flora Garden, the Annual and Perennial Borders, and the Plant Family Collection. In the pages that follow, you'll find numerous inspirational designs for edible gardens created by BBG's expert garden curators.

Gardening with Edible Plants

As Barbara Damrosch makes clear in the next chapter, food plants can be very rewarding in the home garden. Most edibles have been selected to be easy to grow and care for (which is one of the reasons they are so great to grow with children). Annuals offer a quick progression from seed to maturity, meaning in most cases that there will not be long to wait for their peak visual display and edible bounty, and they will change dramatically through the season. Designed to be consumable, edible annuals offer almost immediate visual gratification, after which you can harvest them and try something new—or let them bolt to see familiar plants take on forms you never dreamed of.

Herbaceous perennials return year after year, emerging dramatically from seemingly lifeless soil and, like annuals, rapidly forming vegetative parts. Fruit-bearing woody trees and shrubs may provide less drama over the growing season

Public gardens can provide design inspiration for prospective vegetable growers while modeling practical techniques, as seen in the Herb Garden at Brooklyn Botanic Garden.

but offer structure and year-round visual interest in addition to fragrant spring flowers and tasty payoffs.

The plant encyclopedia that starts on page 50 profiles many of the garden-worthy options featured in this book's sample designs and offers myriad choices for gardeners who wish to incorporate edible plants into their sites. A summary of each plant's origins and cultural or culinary significance is followed by tips on growing, harvesting, and eating it and photographs of the plant's aesthetic features. An "Edible Garden Plants at a Glance" chart (page 108) calls out those species that are native to North America, great for kids (or beginning gardeners of any age) to grow, or that can be productive even in sites that receive less than six hours of sun each day.

There are many books dedicated to the practice of growing edible plants. Our goal in creating this handbook was not to replicate the information contained in other references but to share some of Brooklyn Botanic Garden's own favorite plants and the strategies we use to incorporate them into an ornamental landscape. It offers a quick reference and starting point for additional exploration. We're sure you'll learn something new in these pages, and hope it inspires you to grow an attractive, entertaining, and bountiful edible garden.

Beauty and Bounty in the Garden

Barbara Damrosch

After a half century during which Mr. McGregor's garden became a quaint children's-book concept, Americans are finally growing their own food again. Back-to-the-landers were the first to point the way, followed by foodies drawn by the siren song of heirloom tomatoes. Journalists updated us daily on the unreliability and general scariness of our petroleum-driven diet, and, finally, a steep recession opened a gate that may never be shut again. We don't take food for granted anymore. We're fussy about how it tastes. And if we have a patch of sunny ground, we can produce our own.

Often it's just that: a patch. Yards are smaller and shadier than they were when the victory gardens of World War II rolled out half the nation's vegetable rations. Some eager converts have given their copper beeches a farewell hug and cleared their land for action. But most look for a workable compromise between their yen for fresh food a few steps from the door and the delights of a beautiful, livable landscape. It's a challenge, but an exciting one that's more about creativity than limitation.

The Touchstone Garden

Let's take a look at the traditional American vegetable plot, a long rectangle striped crosswise with neat, parallel rows. In some ways it's a relic of times past, its yields and row spacing based on horse or tractor cultivation. Home gardens are compact now, and we expect to get much more food out of every square foot of soil. But the basic principles behind that old style remain a touchstone. Its purpose is to give annual food crops the best possible advantage, so that they can make rapid, vigorous growth in the proper season. For cool-weather crops such as lettuce and peas, this means spring or fall. For others such as tomatoes and peppers, it's the warm days of summer.

To gain this advantage, a gardener pampers vegetable crops with a soil enriched with plenty of organic matter. A soil test will tell you what minerals you might need to add, but if you have tilled in plenty of compost and well-rotted manure, you're on your way to a good harvest. Organic matter provides many things: fertility, the loose, fluffy structure that plant roots love, and most important of all, soil life. When you add organic matter you are feeding the billions of creatures (most of them invisible bacteria and fungi) that inhabit your garden and do most of the work for you by making nutrients available to plants. These simple lessons can be

Towering above a wave of Tuscan kale (*Brassica oleracea*), stately sunflowers (*Helianthus annuus*) attract the eye—and buzzing pollinators—to other garden flowers too, including the blossoms of squash (*Cucurbita pepo*), peeking out below.

learned just by watching how nature gardens: Leaves fall from the trees, plant and animal matter decay in the earth, and from this springs more life. Having created an incubator of life, all the gardener needs to do is space the plants so that they are free from the competition of weeds—or each other—then keep them watered, staked, or pruned as needed.

Can Practical Gardens Be Beautiful?

If I have learned anything in my years with plants, it's that form follows function. Our eye responds to a soil that looks like rich chocolate cake, to leaves that glow with health, to a garden where nothing looks smothered or stressed. The same things that make a garden grow well also make it beautiful. Given a good start and maintained regularly, it will be satisfying to look at. If chaotic, it will turn anyone away, especially the gardener. In the plots from which my husband and I supply our own kitchen, we stick to a formula of 30-inch-wide beds (easy to reach into but never stepped into) and space-saving 12-inch-wide paths. This design makes weeding easier, and sets a psychological standard of order that keeps us on our toes. Ours is planted in rows, but gardens organized in small squares or blocks are also well suited to modern yards. The effect is a charming patchwork quilt of plants with different foliage shades and textures.

Whatever the garden's layout, the trick is to keep it both productive and beautiful by removing each spent crop and planting something new in its place. Even a small garden can produce an extraordinary amount of food when succession plantings are used. Red peppers, for example, might follow early radishes or lettuce, then give way to garlic. Interplanting, another great trick, allows two crops to overlap: Newly transplanted kale might share a bed with early spinach plants, to be harvested before the later-maturing kale shades them. Most greens can be grown as cut-and-come-again crops, either by cutting them back to the ground and letting them regrow, as with a mesclun mix, or by harvesting a few leaves at a time, as with spinach, beet greens, and Swiss chard. A supply of new lettuce transplants on hand, to pop into empty rows, will also keep the garden looking full and abundant.

Having fun with garden geometry can lead to even more decorative schemes, from circles and triangles to free-form swirls. But bear in mind that each carrot or tomato plant has a minimum amount of space it needs in order to thrive. You may have to choose between the charm of a casual or whimsical garden and a more ordered one that allows you to organize crop rotations to avoid pest and disease buildup, and to accurately plan your yield.

Where to Put the Garden

There is a tendency, when planning a food garden, to consign it to a distant corner, near the compost pile, the toolshed, and the laundry line. As a cook who often darts out the door in mid-sauté to pull a few scallions, I don't want to go that far. A kitchen garden should be handsome enough to view from the terrace, the living

Designing for efficiency—using space and light to the best effect—needn't preclude beauty; trellised vines and mix-and-match cultivar combos add elegance to the symmetry of grids.

room, or even from the street. If the front yard is where the sun is, there the veggies must go. Some neighbors might object, but a few brave and talented food growers could probably change their minds.

Once, just for fun, I planted a vegetable plot in an area of our yard normally reserved for flowers. I nicknamed it Villandry after the huge and outrageously perfect chateau garden in France's Loire Valley, where nary a cabbage is ever picked and eaten for fear of spoiling the design. I set one rule: Each crop had to look good all season and then be removed all at once at the growing season's end. The rows included red cabbages like giant roses, ferny storage carrots, spiky blue-green leeks, strawberry plants, and celery root.

It was a success, but such limits shouldn't be necessary. Sometimes the best way to create a beautiful vegetable picture is just to put a frame around it in the form of an attractive fence. The fence may be there to keep out rabbits, but by adding a well-made decorative gate, and perhaps an arch, it becomes your pride and joy. Need a taller fence to exclude deer? Build it of decorative lattice and use that extra height to grow crops vertically. At various times I have grown cucumbers, tomatoes, tomatillos, Malabar spinach, gourds, small winter squash, peas, and numerous kinds of beans on garden fences. All take up less space this way, are easier to pick, and become the green-clothed walls of a garden room.

Architectural elements like pavers, walls, and containers add year-round interest to the edible garden, define beds, and provide footpaths for easy cultivation and harvesting.

With a fence, as with most garden structures, natural materials lend a harmonious look. A talented artist might turn brightly painted surfaces and even shiny steel into handsome garden artifacts, but wood or iron, and especially rusted iron, may be better at blending when you want the plants themselves to shine. Black is the most unobtrusive color with which to paint, say, a metal post; it recedes into the background more effectively than green. I even use black hoses in our yard, especially when they are placed in a permanent location. When choosing stones I avoid ones that are starkly light in color. Garden aids such as floating row covers and black plastic mulch are sometimes necessary but unattractive evils. But row covers are often temporary, and black plastic is well hidden once the plants grow. Even Rosemary Verey's famous potager at Barnsley House in the English Cotswolds used black plastic to coax peppers to ripeness.

A Color Revolution

If you are still not convinced that edibles can glamorize a garden, look at a recent seed catalog. Gardeners these days are mad for color. Lettuces flounce frilly red-tipped skirts over pale chartreuse petticoats. Cauliflower, which used to come only in basic white, can be deep purple, bright gold, and lime green. Swiss chard mixtures, with rainbow-hued stems and ribs, are as flashy as a row of zinnias. Peppers, eggplants, carrots, and radishes are all exploding with color to brighten up the plate, and often the garden as well. Even a simple planting of four lettuce varieties, with different colors, textures, and forms, can be stunning.

There's nothing frivolous about this trend. It's partly about the rediscovery of old varieties, such as purple carrots and striped tomatoes, that predate modern hybrids and are now part of a growing movement to preserve plant diversity. The colors that draw us to plants are signaling to us about the phytonutrients they contain, the carotenes, lycopenes, betalains, and anthocyanins judged to be beneficial to our health. If you have a choice between growing a red-leafed beet such as 'Bull's Blood' rather than a green one, there is no harm in choosing red for its looks, then planting it next to feathery fennel or deep blue-green Tuscan kale for a dramatic contrast. Many pictures can be painted in the food garden this way, as long as they don't disrupt your crop rotation scheme.

Some vegetables, of course, produce handsome blooms. Okra, before the pods form, has blossoms like small hollyhocks (those of 'Red Burgundy' are especially lovely). Potato plants have beautiful lavender or white flower clusters. Eggplant makes purple trumpets and artichokes neon-violet thistle heads. And it is always worth growing scarlet runner beans for their brilliant flowers, beloved by humming-birds. (We also enjoy the pods as snap beans as well as the shelled seeds.) With brassicas such as broccoli, the appearance of bright clouds of yellow flowers is considered a sign of neglect, since it means the end of production. But not if you are saving

Plant pungent sage (*Salvia* species) and marigold (*Tagetes tenuifolia*) at the edge of the border, where they can be brushed in passing or plucked for spur-of-the-moment garnishes.

seeds. Pay a visit to the display garden at Heritage Farm, the headquarters of the Seed Savers Exchange in Decorah, Iowa, and you'll see all sorts of vegetables in full bloom. The blossomy towers of bolted lettuce alone are worth the trip.

Mixing Ornamentals with Edibles

Nature makes no distinction between the plants we grow for decoration and those we grow for food. Most bloom, then set fruiting bodies for reproduction, and whether we eat them, admire them, or both, is our choice. The more important distinctions for the gardener lie in how those plants grow: whether they are annual or perennial, aggressive or not.

Adding annual flowers to a vegetable garden is easy to do and can produce a wonderful effect. In the little garden I keep just for my own use I often tuck in a few zinnias for cutting, 'Lemon Gem' marigolds for their tasty petals, and sunflowers to attract pollinating bees. Ornamental sweet peas (with their toxic pods) share the fence with edible ones. But all these flowers grow, like the vegetables, in their allotted spaces. Trailing petunias may roam in other parts of the yard, but not here.

The herb garden is a bit more complicated. Perennial herbs such as thyme and sage are fragrant and pretty, and it's no wonder that gardeners arrange them in neat parterres, close to the kitchen door. Thanks to their Mediterranean origin, they look great in rock gardens too, at home in spare, stony soil. Many herbs, especially sages and chives, also have gorgeous flowers, and breeders have lost no time creating showier selections of these and other wild plants such as *Agastache* 'Blue Fortune' (hybrid anise hyssop) and *Origanum vulgare* 'Zorba Red'. I also tuck in some annual herbs such as cilantro and dill, but since they don't compete well with the root systems of perennial herbs, I give the annuals their own space, easily amended with compost each year. Any I need in great quantity, such as basil for pesto, I plant in the vegetable garden.

Vegetables can sometimes be worked into perennial gardens and shrub borders, especially vigorous, dramatic ones such as artichokes or cardoons that can hold their own among tenacious established plantings. Curly parsley and alpine strawberries make a nice front edge. A stand of corn in a large border, as an ornamental grass, is stunning when its tassels are backlit by the sun, but for summer corn roasts you'll want ample backup in the vegetable garden. I've seen asparagus in a shrub border, its ferny foliage glowing golden in fall. I like it even more by itself, along a fence.

The Edible Yard

As long as it's done in a way that is horticulturally sound, I'm for adding as many edibles as possible to urban, suburban, or rural yards, and to public spaces as well. Ask yourself, whenever you're ready to plant a tree, shrub, hedge, or vine, "Could something delicious go here? Each region has its possibilities, whether citrus and figs in California or blueberries and filberts in Maine. Plant a few apple trees for eating and for children to climb. Peach trees bear when just a few years old. Crabapples and

Artfully placed arbors supporting hardy kiwi vines (*Actinidia arguta*) create an intimate garden room filled with trellises and containers of vegetables, herbs, and ornamentals.

plums are perfectly scaled for small yards, nut trees for large ones. Look for wonderful native fruits such as the American persimmon and the pawpaw—a delectable, tropical-tasting gem that can grow almost everywhere. Grow grapes or passion fruit on an arbor above the terrace where you sit. Beautify a stockade fence with festoons of hardy kiwi vines, their leaves splashed white and pink in summer, gold in fall. Create a diverse edible hedgerow, not only for you but also for birds and other wildlife. Fill it with elderberries, serviceberries, blueberries, currants, bush cherries, and beach plums. Few groundcovers are edible, but I've used both sweet potato and pumpkin vines to blanket large areas and keep them weed free.

Don't be afraid to experiment. Rosalind Creasy, the mother of the edible landscaping movement, sows mesclun greens around her spring bulbs to take their place after they bloom. Her book *Edible Landscaping* is full of tips like that. Lee Reich's *Landscaping with Fruits* will inspire you to plant medlars and mulberries. The designs in the pages that follow offer numerous other ideas.

Perhaps someday we will all look at our clipped privets and mown lawns and think, "Wouldn't an edible paradise be more rewarding?" And why not extend that paradise to the grounds of schools, hospitals, nursing homes, libraries, churches, and industrial "parks"? In a time of desperate need or crisis, those places would quickly become our breadbaskets, just as they did in the victory garden days. Why wait?

Edible Garden Designs

There are so many ways to feature edible plants in the garden—you are by no means limited to planting in rigid rows or sequestering all of your vegetable plants to out-of-the-way plots. We asked seven past and current gardeners at Brooklyn Botanic Garden to create designs that highlight the versatility and beauty of edible plants.

Throughout the designs that follow are threaded garden strategies and cultivation tips that will help you grow healthy and productive plants; also included are design tips that will expand your creative palette. Some designs draw upon traditional cultivation models like cottage gardens and potagers; others show how to look to nature for inspiration, for example, by mimicking the layers of a forest. Techniques like espalier, succession planting, and container gardening will help you maximize productivity even in small spaces.

Edible plants like kiwi, asparagus, and sorrel create the framework for the front door in "A Delicious Front Yard." "An Ornamental Potager" shows you how to create a gorgeous and bountiful vegetable garden, and "A Native Food Forest and Meadow" creates a virtual forest of food plants indigenous to the northeastern United States. Gardeners game to try their hand at growing fruit get a solid tutorial in "A Home Orchard." And "Container Gardens" promises plentiful, attractive harvests in even the most constrained places.

Horticultural staff for public parks and gardens as well as community gardeners can glean tips on how to feature food plants in high-traffic areas in "A Public Garden." Parents and educators can look to "A Children's Garden" for ways to help even the youngest gardeners grow their own food while fostering an appreciation of nature.

Each design is accompanied by a specific plant list detailing selections appropriate to the garden's theme and purpose, ranging from great-performing old favorites to showy new cultivars. A drawing indicates how these plants could look together. (Note that, for simplicity's sake, the illustrations include limited numbers of specimens and don't represent an exact moment in time but rather show the features of plants that may bloom and fruit at different times.) You can adapt these designs for your specific garden site—or use them as inspiration for your own creative exploration.

From the leeks (*Allium ampeloprasum* var. *porrum*) near the front of this border to the tasseling corn (*Zea mays*) at the back, almost everything is edible—and gorgeous.

A Delicious Front Yard

Meghan Ray

The edible landscape gives gardeners tangible reward for their effort—what could be better than actually eating the fruits of your labor? But often edible plants are relegated to a vegetable patch, planted in rows, tucked to the side, or pushed to the back of the yard. It's much more efficient—not to mention visually appealing—to incorporate edible plants into the overall design of the home landscape. As I'll show in this design, you can even successfully plant them in that most looked-upon of areas, the front yard.

Plants in the front garden have to live up to certain aesthetic expectations, and the edible plants you put there must provide structure, color, and year-round interest as well as be delicious and easy to grow. A mixed border is an ideal scheme for incorporating edible perennials into a multipurpose landscape since the plants work in combination and support each other to create a cohesive design. Seasonal flowers, along with contrasting plant sizes and foliage textures, boost visual interest.

A Cottage Garden Design

The front-yard cottage garden has long been a place where useful and decorative plants mingle. The term "cottage garden" may bring to mind small, thatched-roof English houses surrounded by lush rosebushes and overflowing beds of hollyhocks and foxgloves—but at their more humble beginnings many centuries ago, cottage gardens were created to supply the home with fresh herbs and vegetables and were much less flower-centric than their modern-day cousins. Ornamental plants did play a role in early cottage gardens but were used to fill in gaps between edible and more practical plants. The front-yard design for this chapter is every bit as useful as those original cottage gardens, with plants that have edible fruits or foliage that also happen to form a welcoming, highly decorative front-yard display.

In one of the most classic cottage-garden styles, the garden is divided by the walk to the front door and is full of edible plants. Here, fig (*Ficus carica*) and juniper (*Juniperus communis*) trees provide a vertical frame for the house. The large, lobed leaves and plump fruits of the fig create an appealing asymmetry with the delicate foliage and small blue-black berries of the juniper. Highbush blueberry plants (*Vaccinium corymbosum*) form bushy, fruit-filled shrubs in front of the fig tree, and asparagus (*Asparagus officinalis*), lovage (*Levisticum officinale*), and winter savory (*Satureja montana*), if unexpected in a front yard, have charming mid-height foliage and flowers. Low-lying creeping raspberry (*Rubus rolfei*) fronts the sidewalk, and an arbor of kiwi (*Actinidia arguta*) beckons visitors up your front walk.

Preparing the Site

Before you put shovel to soil, you'll need to do a bit of research about your site. Survey your front yard for light conditions, as that will go a long way in determining which plants are best suited for the site. Plan ahead for irrigation, based on the average rainfall of your area—does the front of the house have a water spigot? Will you want to use drip irrigation? It is especially important to have your soil tested when growing edible perennials and shrubs, because their extensive root systems and long exposure to the soil cause them to absorb more heavy metals and other contaminants from the soil than will shallow-rooted annuals. Before planting, send a soil sample to a Cooperative Extension agent or testing lab to make sure your plot is safe for growing edibles.

Since the plants in this plan require good drainage, check to make sure your soil is free draining. Do a percolation test by digging a hole at least 18 inches deep and filling it with water. When the first batch of water has drained, fill the hole again. The water should drain away at a rate of one to two inches per hour; any slower and you will need to amend the soil. One trick is to top-dress the bed with a two-inch layer of compost, then chop this into the existing soil to a shovel blade's depth (avoid creating separate layers of soil and compost). Another way to create drainage is to raise the level of the soil in the planting bed an inch or two above the existing grade. Make sure the bed slopes away from the house.

DESIGN AND CULTIVATION TIPS

- Many edible plants have been extensively cultivated to perform best under certain conditions, so it is always a good idea to check with the local Cooperative Extension or nursery to see what plants grow well in your region.

- The flowers of some fruit plants need to be pollinated by another member of their species in order to produce fruit, so in those cases you'll want to plant more than one specimen. For some species, both male and female plants are needed because the male and female flowers occur on different plants. These plants are said to be dioecious. Kiwi vines are an example of a dioecious plant; when purchasing them at a nursery, make sure to buy at least one male and one female plant or your female plant will not set fruit.

- Improve soil health and fertility by incorporating compost into the top layer of soil each year. This can be done any time from fall to early spring. Boost fertility during the growing season by drenching the soil with compost tea made from compost, fish emulsion, and liquid kelp. You can make a quick tea by filling a mesh bag with compost and massaging it in a bucket of fresh water for two to three minutes. Then mix in the fish emulsion and kelp to add extra nutrients.

- To maintain the vigor of edible plants, prune or divide them as needed. For woody plants, thin out old wood to increase fruit production, but take care to leave some year-old wood on those plants that don't fruit on new growth. Many herbaceous perennials benefit from division to keep plants growing well. Lift and divide them every three years.

Spacing of Plants

One benefit of the walkway-divided cottage garden is that it allows good access to the plants for maintenance and harvesting and also provides the opportunity to separate plants with specific cultural needs such as high or low pH. Access is also important within the borders themselves: You'll want to leave more space between plants than in a traditional border planting. The extra space improves air circulation and will help prevent problems from pests and diseases. You can incorporate pavers or flat stones throughout the beds to provide places to step when harvesting and caring for plants.

While many garden vegetables are grown as annuals, using edible perennials and shrubs like the ones in this design helps to maintain the structure and integrity of the design and eliminates the need to replant year after year. Given full sun and soil with good drainage, these durable perennials should last for years with a reasonable amount of prep work and maintenance.

Plants Featured in This Garden

Trees

A *Ficus carica*, fig

B *Juniperus communis*, juniper

Shrubs

C *Rubus rolfei*, creeping raspberry

D *Vaccinium corymbosum*, highbush blueberry

Vines

E *Actinidia arguta*, hardy kiwi

Herbaceous Perennials

F *Allium schoenoprasum*, chives

G *Asparagus officinalis*, asparagus

H *Dianthus caryophyllus*, clove pink

I *Fragaria × ananassa*, garden strawberry

J *Levisticum officinale*, lovage

K *Rumex acetosa*, common sorrel

L *Satureja montana*, winter savory

An Ornamental Potager

Cayleb Long

With distinct attention paid to design and plant selection, an edible garden can be highly ornamental. Combining edible plants with bold features such as richly colored foliage and conspicuous texture creates a garden that will provide both veritable bounty and visual engagement. The following pages offer a design that combines aesthetic appeal, a full season of harvestable crops, and yearlong visual interest—an edible garden that is at once beautiful and functional from spring through summer and from sprout to plate.

Preparation

Before starting any garden, take the time to create a plan. First, assess your site. Observe over several days and at different times the amount of light that comes into the space. Keep in mind that the exposure may change over the course of the season; note surrounding buildings and trees that may block direct light at different times of the year. Assess the availability of water, taking into consideration annual rainfall and the amount of irrigation the plants will need; and have the soil tested to ensure it is free of toxins (see "Design and Cultivation Tips," page 24).

Then you can start thinking about what edible plants to grow. Using quality publications, seed and plant catalogs, and reputable websites, you can learn what plants require for best performance and compare those requirements with the conditions that exist in your garden. It's sometimes possible to adjust existing conditions to accommodate the needs of plants—for example, by raising planting beds so that drainage will be improved, conditioning soil with compost for better fertility and structure, or pruning existing trees and shrubs to allow for more light. But it is sometimes better to select plants that are best suited to your site. Plants grown under unfavorable conditions will quickly go into decline and attract diseases and insect pests that may threaten the rest of the garden.

Among site-appropriate edible plants, choose ones that will please both the eye and the palate. Red-leaf lettuce, rainbow chard, and brightly fruited chile peppers are among many great options for visual display. Choose a purple-pod snap bean over the standard green. Or select romanesco with its fascinating head of twisted peaks instead of more pedestrian-looking cauliflower or broccoli. Keep in mind that this garden will be dynamic: Plant forms will likely change dramatically over the growing season.

Potager Design

I've created here a simple potager, a well-equipped, ornamental kitchen garden with fruits and vegetables, herbs, and edible flowers. This scheme provides the efficiency and accessibility of agricultural rows and groupings and the aesthetic appeal of a symmetrical layout. The four beds are raised to provide excellent drainage, ease of maintenance, and a definite edge to the planting areas. Pathways can be graced with a tightly clipped lawn or pea gravel to bolster clean lines. The inclusion of a simple birdbath or other water feature in the center of the design establishes a focal point and attracts birds and beneficial insects, whose visits will enliven the garden throughout the year.

In this design, the combination of foliage—the deep burgundy of 'Bull's Blood' beets (*Beta vulgaris*), the robust silver leaves of cardoons (*Cynara cardunculus*), and the lacy texture of fennel (*Foeniculum vulgare*)—makes for a striking display. 'Moon and Stars' watermelon (*Citrullus lanatus*), which produces deep green fruits with spots of orange and yellow, contrasts nicely with the red spikes of 'Little Lucy' okra (*Abelmoschus esculentus*), and dark, round 'Brandywine' tomatoes (*Solanum lycopersicum*) mirror the melons' shape.

Aromatic and delicious, herbs are lovely planted in a ring around the water feature. If allowed to flower, they will attract a plethora of pollinators to the potager. You can also incorporate edible flowers like nasturtium and borage to spill over edges and fill spaces between other plants. Both offer a colorful presence in the garden and add flavor to salads and other dishes.

DESIGN AND CULTIVATION TIPS

- Keep in mind that there are cool-season and warm-season edible plants. Warm-season growers like melons and okra may grow slowly in the early spring but will explode in size with warmer summer days and nights. Cool-season plants like lettuce thrive during the cooler months of spring and fall, when they can be direct sown for quick harvest. During the heat of the summer, the same plot can be quickly covered with a mixed cover crop of clover, oats, and vetch. This warm-season cover will act as a living mulch, imparting nitrogen to the soil, and it can be worked into the soil as an amendment in the fall.

- In regions with mild winters, the growing season can be extended through most of the year. By sowing cool-season plants like spinach and other greens in the autumn and employing a simple row cover to protect crops from extreme fluctuations in temperature, you can enjoy a nutritious harvest well into winter.

- When growing edible crops, one would be wise to test the soil for heavy metals, carcinogens, and other toxins. These undesirable elements can be taken up in the living tissue of some plants, where they could be consumed at harvest time. Cooperative Extension labs can test a soil sample, provide analysis, and make recommendations for amendment. Soil remediation or replacement may be necessary, depending on what is found.

- Mulching is an essential practice with most vegetable and ornamental gardens. Mulch aids moisture retention in the soil, reducing the need for irrigation. It also helps regulate soil temperatures, keeping the soil cooler in the summer and insulating it from late and early frosts. A 1- to 2-inch layer of mulch will also inhibit seed germination of weeds. In this potager design, a light organic mulch such as straw, buckwheat hulls, or well-composted organic matter is recommended.

- Avoid rototilling planting beds. Repeated tilling can damage soil structure and create hardpan just below the reach of the tiller's tines, inhibiting good drainage. Try using a garden fork to loosen soil and turn under amendments.

You may also wish to thread some tall, airy annuals like tall verbena (*Verbena bonariensis*) or red tassel flower (*Emilia coccinea*) between your vegetables for added visual interest. Though not edible, these tremendous plants offer vibrant violet and scarlet blossoms all season and also attract beneficial insects. Both plants will self-sow; if seedlings become too profuse, remove the spent flowers before seed has a chance to set.

As the growing season comes to a close, stop harvesting some of the plants and allow them to flower. Flower stalks with robust structure, like those of cardoons, may persist through the winter, creating visual interest and wildlife habitat. Plant debris like leaves and stems left on the surface of the soil become a natural mulch. Breaking down over winter, these residues amend the soil and return to it some of the nutrients used during the growing season.

Plants Featured in This Garden

Bed 1

A *Beta vulgaris* 'Bull's Blood', beet

B *Cynara cardunculus*, cardoon

C *Foeniculum vulgare* subsp. *vulgare* Azoricum group 'Zefa Fino', bulb fennel

Bed 2

D *Brassica oleracea* var. *botrytis* 'Veronica', romanesco

E *Brassica oleracea* 'Nero di Toscana', Tuscan kale

F *Daucus carota* subsp. *sativus* 'Purple Haze', 'Red Samurai', 'Yellowstone', carrots

Herb Circle

O *Coriandrum sativum* 'Calypso', coriander*

P *Mentha spicata*, spearmint

Q *Ocimum basilicum* 'Pistou', globe basil*

Bed 3

G *Cucurbita pepo* 'Yellow Crookneck', yellow summer squash

H *Cucurbita pepo* 'Cocozelle', zucchini

I *Phaseolus vulgaris* 'Kentucky Wonder', garden pole bean (summer)

J *Pisum sativum*, sugar snap pea (spring)*

K *Zea mays* 'Stowell's Sweet', sweet corn

Bed 4

L *Abelmoschus esculentus* 'Little Lucy', red okra

M *Citrullus lanatus* 'Moon and Stars', watermelon

N *Solanum lycopersicum* 'Brandywine', tomato

R *Petroselinum crispum* 'Italian Flat Leaf', parsley

S *Salvia officinalis* 'Tricolor', tricolor sage

T *Thymus serpyllum*, creeping thyme

* Not illustrated

A Native Food Forest and Meadow

Ulrich Lorimer

The benefits of using native plants in the landscape are numerous. Local flora help preserve regional biodiversity and character; they require less watering, being naturally adapted to local rain and drought patterns; and they're innately resistant to indigenous pests and diseases. Native plants are also a valuable source of food—for wildlife and humans. This garden design re-creates the complexity of a forest and woodlands-edge meadow community, using plants native to the Northeast. It's just one example of how you can convert your own backyard into resource-saving and wildlife-friendly habitat that also happens to provide you with a delicious harvest of fruits, greens, nuts, and tubers.

For this small-scale edible landscape, I've chosen a variety of native plants representing distinct environmental niches. They combine to form a layered, forestlike setting, with a canopy of trees, understory trees, shrubs, groundcovers, and vines. In nature, layered habitats like this generate immense benefits for the plants—and in a planted setting, they also create great benefits for the gardener. Fallen leaves from canopy trees form a natural leaf mulch, aiding in water retention and weed prevention. Canopy and taller plants also provide shade to plants below them, mitigating sun damage and wilt. Rainwater is dispersed from higher plants to lower ones in an all-natural drip system, and the abundance of plant life at ground level helps hold water in the soil in addition to inhibiting soil erosion.

Following this natural layered model of planting has the added boon of yielding a more abundant harvest (healthier plants make for longer fruiting seasons and better yields). There's also a dynamic visual appeal to this design, with plants in fruit and flower in different seasons, and differing heights, textures, and colors to draw the eye. To enhance the experience, you can build in a small path with a slight bend to allow visitors a sense of discovery as they move into your backyard forest.

The Plants

Mature canopy tree species like shagbark hickory (*Carya ovata*) and American persimmon (*Diospyros virginiana*) afford shade and shelter to the plants living below. Reaching about 70 feet tall, shagbark hickory is a squirrel magnet, but its sweet-tasting nuts are devoured by people as well, and its wood can be used for delicious smoky barbecues. American persimmon grows to about 30 to 40 feet, and its 2-inch-diameter, round, orange fruits are tasty when fully ripe.

Amassed beneath these stately giants are summer-bearing fruit trees and shrubs whose bounty can be enjoyed right from the bush or savored later as jam, jelly, or compote. Shadbush (*Amelanchier laevis*) lights up the early-spring woodland with its brilliant white flowers, which give way to juicy dark red berries. Pawpaw (*Asimina triloba*) graces the spring woodland garden with deep claret-red flowers before its branches become clothed with bold-textured large leaves up to one foot long. Pawpaw's fruit ripens in the summer to form soft, fragrant, yellow bean-shaped berries up to six inches in size, with a flavor reminiscent of very ripe bananas. This tree grows as a clonal stand in the wild and needs a non-clonal partner; to ensure good fruit production, be sure to plant at least two separate trees.

Perennial favorites of the summer berry-picking season, blueberries and huckleberries flourish in the dappled sunlight beneath the trees. Highbush blueberry (*Vaccinium corymbosum*), lowbush blueberry (*V. angustifolium*), and black huckleberry (*Gaylussacia baccata*) bear heavy loads of berries, but don't wait too long to pick them, as local birds and wildlife will gobble them up as soon as they are ripe.

Forming the herbaceous layer underneath and around the shrub and tree plantings are a multitude of spring and summer producers. Early spring brings the most choice of all wild onions, the ramp, or wild leek (*Allium triccocum*), whose tender shoots and bulbs are highly prized by gourmands. Springtime also brings the young edible

GROWING TIPS

- In forests, soil is naturally slightly acidic with lots of loose organic matter. The natives in this design are easy to cultivate and generally tolerant of average to rich soil conditions. Blueberries and huckleberries, however, are happiest with slightly acidic, well-drained soil.

- To maximize productivity in small garden spaces, select plants to occupy each of the vertical layers: canopy (tall trees), understory (small trees, shrubs, vines), and floor (herbaceous plants). Learn about each species' natural habitat and use this information to choose plants that match well with your site conditions.

- For gardeners outside the Northeast, perhaps this design can serve as inspiration to investigate native edible plants in your own region. Local wildflower societies and Cooperative Extensions can help you come up with lists of local natives and nurseries that specialize in native plants and provide sample designs for your own layered, edible landscape.

fiddleheads, or crosiers, of the ostrich fern (*Matteuccia struthiopteris*) and the sweet succulent fruit of the wild strawberry (*Fragaria virginiana*).

Planted at the edge of the path, wintergreen (*Gaultheria procumbens*) and wild ginger (*Asarum canadense*) form dense mats of foliage. The long horizontal rootstock of wild ginger can be cooked and candied or dried and used as a substitute for commercial ginger. Young leaves and fruit of wintergreen can be gathered and used in salads or steeped to make a refreshing herbal tea.

At the edge of the tree canopy, where sun meets shade, is a matrix of meadow wildflowers with several edible attributes. Known as sunchokes in local farmers' markets, the tubers of Jerusalem artichoke (*Helianthus tuberosus*) can be used in place of potatoes in any recipe. Steep the leaves of giant blue hyssop (*Agastache foeniculum*) or wild bergamot (*Monarda fistulosa*) for a relaxing herbal tea. Wild rye (*Elymus virginicus*) offers texture and scale. Lastly, trained onto an arbor or fence, fox grape (*Vitis labrusca*) bears sweet but somewhat seedy grapes throughout summer into fall.

Harvesting the bountiful fruits of this garden is made possible thanks to the pollination services provided by local insects. Without them, plants would not be able to reproduce and create seed. The layered complexity and three dimensionality of this garden provide a myriad of habitats for moths, butterflies, and bees, and the succession of blooms provides pollen and nectar resources from spring through fall. By adding a small beehive, you can put these industrious fliers to work on your behalf. Could there be anything sweeter than your own honey drizzled over the fruits of your native plants?

Plants Featured in This Garden

Canopy Trees

A *Carya ovata*, shagbark hickory

B *Diospyros virginiana*, persimmon

Understory Trees, Shrubs, and Vines

C *Amelanchier laevis*, shadbush

D *Asimina triloba*, pawpaw

E *Gaylussacia baccata*, black huckleberry

F *Vaccinium angustifolium*, lowbush blueberry

G *Vaccinium corymbosum*, highbush blueberry

H *Vitis labrusca*, fox grape

Forest Perennials

I *Allium tricoccum*, wild leek, ramp

J *Asarum canadense*, wild ginger

K *Fragaria virginiana*, wild strawberry

L *Gaultheria procumbens*, wintergreen

M *Matteuccia struthiopteris*, ostrich fern

Meadow Perennials

N *Agastache foeniculum*, giant blue hyssop

O *Elymus virginicus*, wild rye

P *Helianthus tuberosus*, Jerusalem artichoke

Q *Monarda fistulosa*, wild bergamot

A Home Orchard

Joan McDonald

Growing your own fruit and sharing it with others yields a special sense of pride and satisfaction. But becoming an accomplished backyard orchardist takes a lot of physical work—training and pruning the plants, performing pest and disease management—in addition to careful preparation and research. Successful fruit growing requires skills that are honed over time, but there are plenty of fruits that beginning gardeners can have good success with.

The method I follow in growing fruit, and the basis for my design in this chapter, is backyard orchard culture, also known as high-density planting. It's a technique that uses the least amount of space and creates a succession of yield times. The idea is to plant fruit trees close together and prune them to the desired shape or size. Some people choose to espalier against a wall or fence (as I do here with the pears, raspberries, and grapes) so that the fruit only takes up a width of two or three feet. Others plant a hedge to create a type of wall or barrier. And some gardeners choose to plant multiple trees—up to four!—in one hole. The objectives of backyard orchard culture are to have a prolonged harvest of tree-ripe fruit from a small space, to have many fruit varieties planted close together, and to keep the trees small through summer pruning.

Planning the Backyard Orchard

My advice is to grow the kind of fruit you like to eat. All of the plants in my design are personal favorites that are hardy in Zones 6 and 7, with some hardy to Zones 4 and 5. Plants in containers need to be treated as hardy in one zone lower (for example, a gardener in Zone 6 should seek container specimens hardy to Zone 5). Beginners should choose fruit species that have strong constitutions and are easy to grow, like apples, strawberries, blueberries, blackberries, raspberries, and figs. Peaches are somewhat more difficult to master. Sweet cherries and pears are the hardest to grow.

The best guarantee of success with fruiting trees and shrubs is to start with stock that already has a substantial root system. (Inexperienced orchardists are advised to use container-grown plants rather than bare-root saplings.) Another tip is to use dwarf trees that reach 8 to 12 feet in height. Small trees yield crops of manageable size and are much easier to spray, thin, prune, and harvest than large trees. A good rule of thumb for size: No home fruit tree should be taller than the gardener can stand with hands held straight up in the air, unless you want to be inundated with fruit.

Choose self-pollinating tree varieties to eliminate the need to plant two or more of the same type of tree. In many climates, planting more varieties of pears, apples, plums, or cherries can mean better cross-pollination and more consistent production. The pears, apples, and passion vine in my design need to be cross-pollinated to produce fruit. While blueberries are considered self-fertile, you'll get a better crop if you cross-pollinate two different cultivars. The peach, cherry, raspberries, and strawberries I have chosen are self-pollinating.

Most fruits are susceptible to pests and diseases, so look for selections that are disease resistant. It is possible to grow fruit using organic methods by setting up a diligent spraying program using a combination of horticultural oils, organic fungicides, insecticidal soaps, and biological controls like pheromone traps to lure insects to their doom. See the Brooklyn Botanic Garden handbook *Natural Insect Control* for specific strategies.

Planting and Spacing

Choose a location with as much summer sun as possible and soil with good drainage. Fruit plants also require some form of protection from strong wind that still allows for good air circulation.

Your orchard does not have to be planted in rows like a commercial orchard. You can plant trees along a fence or driveway, or place them as part of an overall landscape design, but you do need to allow enough room around each plant for it to grow to its full size. My design is a formal one, and I have left enough room in between plants to maintain them properly. You can also grow many fruits in containers (see above).

Maintenance

The biggest mistake beginning fruit growers make is failing to prune enough. Pruning fruit trees stimulates shoot growth, controls the size and shape of the tree, and improves the quality of the fruit. Thinning the fruit is important too, especially in the tree's early years while it is developing good root and branch structures. Young trees should have 75 percent of the crop removed. Pruning at the same time as thinning is highly recommended. Seeing where the tree sets fruit (on one-year-old wood, two-year-old wood, spurs, etc.) helps you make better pruning decisions.

Home orchards need regular, deep irrigation. A soaker hose or drip irrigation is the best watering method. How often you water depends on your weather, amount of rainfall, and soil type. As a general rule, apply plant-specific organic fertilizers every six weeks during the spring and summer.

Harvesting

In this design, the strawberries and raspberries are the first to ripen in June. Cherries, blackberries, and blueberries follow in July. August begins the parade of apricots, plums, peaches, grapes, and the 'Moonglow' pears. The 'Seckel' dwarf pears, figs, and first apples ripen in early September, and other cultivars ripen through the fall months. With careful planning you can have fresh fruit for a six-month period.

Keep in mind that wildlife will love your fruit just as much as you do. You'll need to protect your bounty from wildlife by using different techniques, netting being the most useful.

Plants Featured in This Garden

Trees and Shrubs

A *Prunus avium* 'Stella', sweet cherry

B *Prunus persica* 'Dwarf Elberta', peach

C *Vaccinium corymbosum* 'Bluecrop',
highbush blueberry

D *Vaccinium corymbosum* 'Herbert',
highbush blueberry

Containers

E *Ficus carica* 'Brown Turkey', fig

F *Malus domestica* 'Golden Sentinel', apple

G *Malus domestica* 'Northpole', apple

H *Fragaria* × *ananassa* 'Honeoye',
garden strawberry

I *Fragaria* × *ananassa* 'Tribute',
garden strawberry

Vines and Espalier-Trained Trees and Shrubs

J *Passiflora incarnata*, passion vine

K *Pyrus communis* 'Seckel', pear

L *Pyrus communis* 'Moonglow', pear

M *Rubus idaeus* 'Heritage', red raspberry

N *Rubus frutiosus* 'Ouachita', blackberry

O *Vitis vinifera* 'Lakemont', grape

P *Vitis vinifera* 'Suffolk Red', grape

Container Gardens

Jennifer Williams

Not all edible plants have to grow in the ground. Given the right conditions, most of the fruits, vegetables, and herbs in this book can be grown in pots, window boxes, or hanging baskets on balconies, rooftops, or small patios. Pots can be incorporated into larger, more traditional backyard spaces as well. Container gardening allows all gardeners, from apartment dwellers to house owners, to create eye-catching themed designs that deliver prolific, delectable harvests.

Combining edible plants in a container design is a great way to get started growing food on a manageable scale—or to try your luck with unfamiliar species. Food plants can be inexpensive and provide quick gratification; and when you tire of a design, it's time to harvest your crops and explore a new idea. Moderate-size containers can be moved indoors over the winter, or tucked into sheltered spaces to take advantage of microclimates, for example, by employing the radiant heat from a south-facing stone wall to extend the growing season.

Following my designs, you can dedicate a container to Southern comfort foods like strawberry-rhubarb pie, or cultivate a Mexican mole container with all the necessary flavorings for a spicy, south-of-the-border menu. Or use these ideas as inspiration for your own inventions—nowadays there are heaps of cultivars specifically bred for containers (dwarf varieties, especially) and edible plants that are every bit as pretty as their ornamental cousins.

When planning a container, think about your culinary and aesthetic goals. It can be useful to adopt a theme, whether it's foods that go well together or plants of a specific color palette. The most pleasing containers convey both structure and lush abandon. One way to jump-start your creativity is to choose a specimen plant as a focal point, for example, a species offering a strong vertical line, particularly vivid color, or interesting leaf shape. Build your other selections around this plant—and have fun!

Think about sizes, textures, and fragrances when you research your plant choices. Also bear in mind how long it takes for your plants to produce their edible parts, particularly if you are looking to harvest them together. Pay careful attention to the specific cultural needs of each plant, grouping plants with, say, similar soil pH requirements together.

In the cultural tips on the next page, I spell out some general rules for growing edible plants in containers. Experiment with your own favorite plants and different types of containers to come up with novel ways to grow your own food.

A lovely edible landscape (or windowsill) is easy to establish and will last the entire growing season if you provide the basics: good soil, sunlight, and moisture.

DESIGN AND CULTIVATION TIPS

- Choose a pot that pleases you. You can use almost any type of container for food gardening, but make sure it has at least one drainage hole in the bottom. Clay, stone, and concrete pots age well and are heavy—good for stability, bad for portability. Lighter materials such as plastic, fiberglass, and metal are portable, will hold moisture longer, and withstand winter freezes.

- Do not fill your containers with soil straight from the garden. It may carry diseases and pests or have poor soil structure for container growing. Instead, fill containers with a sterilized commercial mix for flowering plants and vegetables and add slow-release fertilizer pellets (NPK 20-20-20, to feed the plants for six to eight months). You can also add an organic fertilizer or compost. Do not add composted manure, which can burn plants and impede drainage.

- Here's a helpful equation to use to determine the amount of soil to purchase per container. Bagged soil is sold in cubic feet, and 1 cubic foot equals 6.42 dry gallons. If, for example, you're planting in a half–whiskey barrel (30 gallons), you will need about two large bags of commercial soil mix (2.8 cubic feet per bag).

- Container plants tend to need more frequent watering than those in the ground because their root systems are more limited and because the containers themselves absorb heat and dry out the soil. Water the container whenever the first inch of soil feels dry; check daily in the summer. Water thoroughly, using a gentle spray nozzle, until water runs from the drainage hole. Add hydrogel granules to the soil before planting if you don't think you can keep up with daily watering checks.

- Adequate drainage is essential in container gardening—waterlogged plants will die from lack of oxygen to the roots. Cut a piece of window screen to fit the bottom of the container to help hold in the soil and speed up drainage.

Tips for Specific Plants

- Trim cilantro and chives frequently with scissors; cut them nearly to the base to promote new growth, which is more flavorful and aromatic.

- Pinch basil tips back throughout the summer to encourage leafing and prevent blossoms. The leaves become bitter after flowering, so wait until late in the season to enjoy the attractive and fragrant flowers.

- Perennial plants (marked with an asterisk on the plant lists) can live from year to year. Before the first frost, bring the pineapple plant indoors, and cut back perennials to 3 or 4 inches above the soil line. Place outdoor containers in a sheltered spot protected from the wind and cover them with evergreen boughs. Water the containers when the weather is dry and the temperature above freezing.

- The cardamom plant prefers consistently moist soil, so plant it in its own smaller pot nestled within the large container and use a heavier mix with more organic material like mushroom compost or bark. When the weather cools in fall, take the cardamom out and move it in its pot to a well-lit spot indoors, keeping the temperature above 65°F. Keep the soil evenly moist and mist occasionally through the winter.

Two-Season Potager

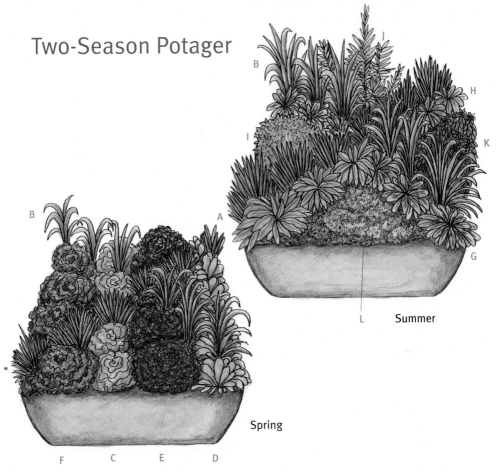

Spring

Summer

Traditional French potagers mingle vegetables, herbs, and cutting flowers in highly ornamental arrangements. With this design, you can grow delicious French cultivars of lettuce, shallots, leeks, and herbs in one eight-gallon terra-cotta pot (19 × 19 × 7 **inches**). Follow the patterns shown in the illustrations to achieve a sculptural appearance and re-create a little plot of Versailles. Leeks and shallots go in in spring and stay all summer. Harvest the cool-season lettuces once summer begins, replacing them with herbs, and plant sorrels next to the alliums along the diagonals.

Plants Featured in This Container

Spring

A *Allium cepa* var. *aggregatum* 'French Red', red shallot

B *Allium ampeloprasum* var. *porrum* 'Bleu de Solaise', leek

C *Lactuca sativa* 'Brune d'Hiver', lettuce

D *Lactuca sativa* 'Gotte Jaune d'Or', lettuce

E *Lactuca sativa* 'Lollo Rosso Dark', lettuce

F *Lactuca sativa* 'Rouge Grenobloise', lettuce

Summer

G *Rumex sanguineus*, blood sorrel

H *Rumex scutatus* 'Silver Buckler', French sorrel

I *Anthriscus cerefolium* 'Great Green', chervil

J *Artemisia dracunculus* 'Sativa', French tarragon*

K *Ocimum basilicum* 'Marseillais', French basil

L *Thymus vulgaris* 'Narrow Leaf French', thyme*

* Perennial

Mexican Mole Mix

Plant some Oaxaca on your front doorstep: This Mexican mole container, filled with tomatillos, jalapeño and habanero chile peppers, and cilantro, cumin, and other herbs, offers a burst of vibrant colors and flavors. You'll need a large container (25 gallon, 23 × 17 inches) and full sun.

Plants Featured in This Container

A *Allium tuberosum*, garlic chives *

B *Capsicum annuum* 'Ancho 101', pepper

C *Capsicum chinense* 'Chocolate Habanero', pepper

D *Capsicum annuum* 'Purple Jalapeño', pepper

E *Coriandrum sativum* 'Slo-Bolt', coriander

F *Cuminum cyminum*, cumin (at rear)

G *Ocimum basilicum* 'Mexican Spice', cinnamon basil

H *Physalis philadelphica* 'Toma Verde', tomatillo

I *Solanum lycopersicum* 'Chocolate Cherry', chocolate cherry tomato

* Perennial

Southern Pickle Tubs (plus Dessert)

The Southern comfort foods collards, mustard greens, and sweet potatoes grow alongside Vidalia onions in the cool season, while all the makings for great pickles—okra, dill, and cucumbers—flourish in the summer heat. Finish off your meal with a slice of pie made from your strawberry-rhubarb dessert tub. For the warm-season plants, use a 25-inch tub; for cool-season plants, 21 inches; and for dessert, 17 inches.

Plants Featured in These Containers

Dessert

A *Fragaria × ananassa* 'Ozark Beauty', strawberry*

B *Rheum rhabarbarum* 'Crimson Red', rhubarb*

Cool Season

C *Allium cepa* 'Yellow Granex', Vidalia onion

D *Brassica juncea* 'Southern Giant Curled', mustard greens

E *Brassica oleracea* var. *acephala* 'Georgia Southern Circle', collards

F *Ipomoea batatas* 'Vardaman', sweet potato

Warm Season

G *Abelmoschus esculentus* 'Aunt Hetties Red', okra

H *Allium tuberosum*, garlic chives*

I *Anethum graveolens* 'Bouquet', dill

J *Cucumis sativus* 'Homemade Pickles', cucumber

K *Solanum lycopersicum* 'Spears Tennessee Green', tomato

* Perennial

A Container for Shade

Most food plants require full sun and lots of it, but some more forgiving species will tolerate—and even thrive—in shadier conditions. This collection of shade-friendly edibles forms a pleasing blend of colors, heights, and textures and will help stock your kitchen with yummy fresh herbs and vegetables. For a dash of color, mix in shade-loving edible flowers like violets (*Viola* species). Use a 25-gallon container measuring 27 × 30 inches.

Plants Featured in This Container

A *Allium cepa × proliferum*, walking onion *

B *Elettaria cardamomum*, cardamom

C *Matteuccia struthiopteris*, ostrich fern *

D *Melissa officinalis*, lemon balm *

E *Mentha × piperita*, peppermint *

F *Mentha spicata*, spearmint *

* Perennial

Dark Delights

Spring

Summer

For a contrast to green hues, plant these purple, red, and blue-green edibles. As with the potager planter, you can harvest the cool-season greens (kale and mustards) to transition to summer with pineapple, pepper, and purple sage to accompany the beets and fennel. Use a 23-gallon container (39 × 17 × 15 inches).

Plants Featured in This Container

Spring

A *Beta vulgaris* 'Bull's Blood', beet
B *Brassica oleracea* 'Lacinato', Tuscan kale
C *Brassica juncea* 'Osaka Purple', mustard greens
D *Brassica juncea* 'Red Giant', mustard greens
E *Foeniculum vulgare* 'Smokey', bronze fennel*

Summer

F *Ananas comosus*, pineapple
G *Capsicum annuum* 'Black Pearl', pepper
H *Ipomoea batatas* 'Blackie', sweet potato
I *Ocimum basilicum* 'Red Rubin', basil
J *Salvia officinalis* 'Purpurescens', sage*

* Perennial

A Public Garden

Caleb Leech

Visitors to public gardens often look to be wowed by flowers and bright colors. Public culinary gardens, with their humbler, backyard origins, have to work a bit harder to impress. For practical reasons, vegetable gardens follow a common scheme, and row upon row of eggplants, tomatoes, and cucumbers all generally resemble each other. To elicit the interest of garden visitors, the plantings must show flair and perhaps a touch of the exotic. To invite visitors in to interact with the exhibit, gardeners have to employ smart designs that are both appealing to the eye and able to withstand the passage of many feet. In this chapter, I've devised a sample food garden design for a public garden, based on my experience as curator of the Herb Garden at Brooklyn Botanic Garden.

The Main Plantings

Taller plants are generally located toward the back of a border, but this shouldn't be viewed as a set rule. Pulling some of the taller plants forward in the beds can lend more depth to the planting. In the design I've created, Joseph's coat (*Amaranthus tricolor*) and plumed cockscomb (*Celosia argentea*) rise from amid the other plants. These close relatives each provide flamboyant color—Joseph's coat has dramatic yellow-and-red edible leaves and plumed cockscomb bright crimson flower plumes. Plumed cockscomb maintains a wispier, airier form while Joseph's coat lends a bulkier presence. These tall plants also serve to provide shade to plants that would otherwise languish in the hot summer sun. Here, rhubarb (*Rheum rhabarbarum*) and woodland strawberry (*Fragaria vesca*) thrive in the partial shade.

Cardoon (*Cynara cardunculus*) is a spectacular structural plant with bold, felted silver-gray leaves. Rock samphire (*Crithmum maritimum*) has succulent foliage and creamy umbel-type flowers with a subtle beauty. When these two lesser-known perennials flank each other, the result is distinctive and somewhat exotic. A sweep of aristocratic Tuscan kale (*Brassica oleracea* 'Lacinato'), with its dark blue-green leaves, contrasts particularly nicely with the vibrant plants edging the bed.

Edges

Establishing sharp and clean edges is often the easiest, quickest way to tighten up a garden. It also serves to frame and guide a visitor's experience of the plants. In a public garden, this is even more important due to heavy foot traffic and the danger careless steps pose to displays. During heavily trafficked periods, I often resort to stringing a jute fence between bamboo stakes to remind visitors to stick to the path. Another solution is to weave temporary wattle fences, a fun activity for garden volunteers and interns. Late winter or early spring is an excellent time to prune back many shrubs, providing plenty of material for weaving a short fence. Depending on availability, many shrub cuttings can be particularly ornamental. Red- and yellow-stemmed dogwoods, different willow species, and birch twigs all provide a variety of colorful material.

In this design, I've chosen a combination of bright, sturdy, and fragrant plants to clearly mark the edges of the bed, withstand foot traffic, and release fragrant warnings to visitors to be mindful of the display. An interplanting of French sorrel (*Rumex scutatus*) and Thai basil (*Ocimum basilicum* 'Siam Queen') combines a visual border of flowers and foliage with a vigorous growth habit and strong fragrance. Thai basil is a robust but neat grower and possesses a mouthwatering anise scent. Its mulberry-colored flower bracts are particularly showy held above the deep green and purple foliage. Low-growing French sorrel is a long-lived perennial that rebounds easily from abuse. It's a favorite of children who love the mouth-puckering, tart flavor of the ruffled, lime-green triangular leaves.

Scrambling nasturtium (*Tropaeolum* species) should never be overlooked in an edible garden, and it works quite well as an edging plant. With a profusion of flowers and rounded, slightly scalloped leaves bearing pronounced silver veins, nasturtium is a vigorous plant that can quickly overflow the edges of a border, imparting an organic shape to the bed. Nasturtium habits may be mounding, vining, trailing, or sprawling;

DESIGN AND CULTIVATION TIPS

- At least five to six hours of full sunlight is needed for this garden to flourish. Generally, the more sun, the healthier the plants will be. If the site has shade issues, the gardener will have to be more vigilant, for when the plants are stressed due to lack of sun, they tend to be choice targets of unwanted pests (which may necessitate the judicious use of organic sprays and other management).

- The plants in this design are outstanding performers from all types of climates and garden conditions. If there is adequate sunlight, most other issues pertaining to the site can be remedied with a little work. A light, well-draining sandy loam is ideal. If the soil is too heavy, raised beds will help alleviate drainage issues. If it is overly sandy, the addition of organic material in the form of compost or well-rotted manure will aid in water and nutrient retention.

for border edges I generally choose a trailing type. It shrugs off abuse, even bouncing back from aphid infestations and subsequent high-powered blasts from the garden hose. If a few stems are crushed, it will rapidly fill back in.

An interplanting of signet marigolds (*Tagetes tenuifolia*) and golden oregano (*Origanum vulgare* 'Aureum') provides a bright edging. The delicate ferny leaves of the signet marigold belie its ease of culture: Seeds sown in the spring germinate quickly and form neat bushes bright with tiny yellow and orange flowers that can be tossed in a salad for a touch of color. Golden oregano rapidly spreads to form a bright groundcover, rooting wherever it touches the ground.

Garden Interpretation

Clearly labeled plants change a public garden from a purely aesthetic experience to an educational one. In Brooklyn Botanic Garden's Herb Garden, each species is given a label with its scientific and common names, region of origin, family, and a concise and interesting story about the plant. I've seen teachers base lesson plans for school groups around the text found on our plant labels—indeed, plants can offer lessons in subjects ranging from history and anthropology to botany and language, and more. In the Herb Garden we often include entertaining cultural stories on our signs, like the superstitious belief that fennel wards off witches; other labels offer culinary tips or short botany lessons.

Public gardens are excellent forums for the exchange of ideas and new inspiration. The gardener should always strive to broaden visitors' knowledge of plants in addition to appealing to their aesthetic tastes.

Plants Featured in This Garden

Annuals

A *Amaranthus tricolor*, Joseph's coat

B *Brassica oleracea* 'Lacinato', Tuscan kale

C *Celosia argentea*, plumed cockscomb

D *Crithmum maritimum*, rock samphire

F *Origanum vulgare* 'Aureum', golden oregano

G *Rumex scutatus*, French sorrel

H *Tagetes tenuifolia*, signet marigold

I *Tropaeolum* species, nasturtium

Herbaceous Perennials

J *Cynara cardunculus*, cardoon

K *Fragaria vesca*, woodland strawberry (not seen)

L *Ocimum basilicum* 'Siam Queen', Thai basil

M *Rheum rhabarbarum*, rhubarb

A Children's Garden

Ashley Gamell

Plant a bean seed with children, and you open up new worlds for them. For a child—and for most adults—sowing a seed, tending it, and watching the plant grow from week to week is a source of amazement, providing countless opportunities for firsthand learning, evoking a sense of stewardship, and sparking an appreciation of nature. All the better when you can eat that plant, too: An edible garden can be a haven of joy and exploration for kids.

When planning an edible children's garden, whether for a school, home, or community setting, you want always to keep the special needs and imaginations of children in mind. Invite your young participants to be fully involved in the gardening, so that they feel a deep interest and ownership in their plantings. This chapter's farm-inspired design incorporates favorites from Brooklyn Botanic Garden's historic Children's Garden and features plants that present special opportunities for discovery.

Small Hands Do Big Work

Children learn more and feel more invested in the garden if they participate in every step of the process, from dreaming up the garden plan to baking the zucchini bread. Tougher tasks like sowing, staking, and harvesting will require close guidance, and young children will need assistance with projects that test fine motor skills, like thinning crowded seedlings. More general tasks such as mounding soil beds, mulching, weeding, and raking allow children to become absorbed in the work on their own.

Choose tools that will be easy and safe for children to handle. Lightweight, child-size tools with smaller grips allow kids to work comfortably. Most crops can be harvested by hand, though safety scissors make a nice stand-in for pruners when needed. The single greatest tool in a children's garden is a child-size watering can. Children love to water plants by hand, and it cultivates in them a real sense of caretaking. It will be necessary to supplement with a thorough soak from a sprinkler or hose on a gentle shower setting—and small gardeners will enjoy being sprinkled by the hose themselves on hot summer days.

The Garden Plan

To make the space special, and safe, for children, incorporate vertical elements like tall borders and trellises that mark off the perimeters and create child-sized nooks. This chapter's design includes a bean teepee large enough for a few children to crawl into, a raspberry hedge that forms a barrier along the street side, and a row of giant sunflowers that creates a natural northern border. (Both sunflowers and raspberries attract wildlife that kids will enjoy watching.) Have children make and decorate plant labels, signs, and ornaments to make the space their own.

Choose crops that will work best within the time frame of the children's involvement, so that they are able to harvest at least some of what they've sown. For school gardens that lie fallow in summer, cherry tomatoes and other warm-weather fruits should be waived in favor of cool-season crops that mature quickly, like greens and root vegetables. Read seed packets to see how many days a crop requires for harvest, and plant ones that are likely to succeed in the time you have.

This design is for a three-season garden, with many of the plants producing continuously from spring through fall. Impatient spring gardeners can harvest fledgling carrots, beets, and lettuce as baby roots and greens. "Cut-and-come-again" leaf lettuce, Tuscan kale, and chard provide a full season of bounty, as you can repeatedly harvest older leaves and leave new ones to grow. Several rounds of lettuce, carrots, and beets can be sown and harvested over the course of the growing season. *Lactuca sativa* 'Black Seeded Simpson' is a versatile lettuce cultivar with frilly lime-green leaves that make it through three seasons. Tomatoes and zucchini arrive with summer, followed by colorful Indian corn. Tuscan kale and everbearing raspberries are the marathon runners, producing from early summer straight through frost.

DESIGN AND CULTIVATION TIPS

- The beds in this design are mounded a few inches above the path level. Raised beds drain well, are easily distinguished from walkways, and are comfortable for children to work in. In planning the size of raised beds, keep in mind the reach of a child's arm: Very small children can reach the center of a bed that is one to two feet wide; bigger kids can comfortably work with a space up to four feet wide.

- In a garden shared by many, it is best to choose prolific fruits and vegetables that can be easily distributed rather than plants that provide just one or two prizewinners a season. Particularly in a small space, forego pumpkins and eggplants in favor of finger foods like snap peas and berries. Encourage your young gardeners to eat their harvest fresh whenever possible. Even corn and beets, finely grated, can be enjoyed without any preparation. Send some crops home to be shared proudly at the family table. Harvest and clean any surplus and deliver it to a local soup kitchen.

- To reduce weeds, sheet mulch by spreading a layer of newspaper on the raised bed, then cover with several inches of fine mulch or compost, into which you will plant your crops. The newspaper will discourage latent weeds from growing. By the end of the growing season, the paper will have decomposed. Replace the paper and renew the soil with compost at the start of each spring.

Kids love color, so brighten your design with outlandish heirlooms and seed mixes of colorful cultivars. 'Chioggia' beets (*Beta vulgaris*) can be sliced open to reveal candy-striped rings of red and white. The multicolored stems of 'Bright Lights' chard (*Beta vulgaris* var. *cicla*) light up beds with orange, pink, purple, white, and yellow stalks. 'Jewel Mix' nasturtiums (*Tropaeolum majus*) trail wonderfully from containers or make lush mounds as an edging.

All of the plants in this design can be sown directly into the garden as seeds, except the basil and tomatoes, which should be started indoors in late winter. Children can start them in egg cartons with drainage holes pricked in the bottoms and watch them grow on a sunny windowsill before transplanting them into the garden beds in early summer. By midsummer, the cherry tomato plants are covered in sweet red gems perfect for eating off the vine. After harvesting the basil, children can make pesto on the spot with a dash of salt and olive oil in a hand-cranked food processor.

Some plants earn their space in this garden because of the teachable moments they provide. Gardeners must discern the male zucchini flowers from the females before frying up the tasty (male) blossoms, and can learn to hand pollinate them for better squash production. Some sunflower heads can be cut for their nutritious seeds, while others can be left for visiting squirrels and goldfinches. Corn, beans, and squash can be planted together as the "three sister" crops that Native Americans subsisted on. Kids can observe a complete plant life cycle by collecting seeds from many of these plants, then cleaning, storing, and planting them the next year.

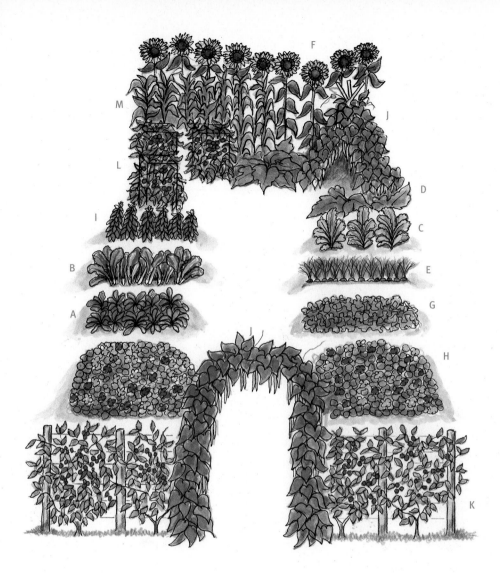

Plants Featured in This Garden

A *Beta vulgaris* 'Chioggia', beet

B *Beta vulgaris* var. *cicla* 'Bright Lights', chard

C *Brassica oleracea* 'Nero di Toscana', Tuscan kale

D *Cucurbita pepo* 'Spacemiser', zucchini

E *Daucus carota* subsp. *sativus* 'Rainbow', carrot mix

F *Helianthus annuus* 'Mammoth Grey Stripe', sunflower

G *Lactuca sativa* 'Black Seeded Simpson', lettuce

H *Tropaeolum majus* 'Jewel Mix', nasturtium

I *Ocimum basilicum* 'Genovese', basil

J *Phaseolus vulgaris* 'Marvel of Venice', garden pole bean

K *Rubus idaeus* 'Heritage', raspberry

L *Solanum lycopersicum* 'Chadwick', cherry tomato

M *Zea mays* 'Painted Mountain', Indian corn

Encyclopedia of Edible Garden Plants

Joni Blackburn

This encyclopedia highlights popular and unusual vegetable and fruit plants whose beauty and structural appeal make them excellent choices for decorative garden landscapes. Interplanted among traditional sun-loving ornamentals like aster, verbena, and gaura, food plants like Tuscan kale, scarlet runner bean, and amaranth blur the distinction between eye candy and wholesome victuals.

Making the transition from purely decorative to edible is not difficult: Aromatic herbs such as lavender, creeping thyme, and bronze fennel are already established stars of front yard borders and terrace containers, along with chives, artichokes, and miniature chile pepper cultivars. Take it a step further and replace ornamental *Allium* 'Globemaster' with palatable relatives like lovely white-flowered garlic chives (*Allium tuberosum*) and decorative sages with multitasking *Salvia officinalis* 'Tricolor' and 'Purpurascens'—attractive and tasty.

Many of the vegetables and fruits described here have cultural requirements typical of vegetable garden plants—fertile, well-draining soil with a slightly acidic pH, at least six hours of full sun a day, and regular moisture. Most are annuals or tender perennials. Some have long growing seasons and either need to be started indoors before the last frost or receive protection from frost toward the end of the season; seed packets and plant labels usually have specific instructions for planting, care, and harvest times.

Browse this encyclopedia for inspiration, and then peruse your seed catalogs and local nurseries for plants best suited for your region and garden situation. Visit www.arborday.org/media/zones.cfm for a recently updated map of USDA hardiness zones. Another great source of information, particularly regarding fruit trees, shrubs, and brambles, as well as plant pest control, is your local Cooperative Extension Service.

Shapely, broad-leafed rosettes of kale and collards (**Brassica oleracea** varieties) and frilly bright lettuce (**Lactuca sativa**) are set off by colorful cultivars of coleus (**Solenostemon** species) in this mixed border of edibles and ornamentals.

Alliums

Nearly as pretty as their purely decorative relatives, chives, onions, garlic, and leeks provide delights for both the eyes and the palate. Alliums offer a variety of decorative charms to the garden, from the sprightly clumps of grasslike chives to the fanning blue-green straps of leeks and fanciful curls of garlic scapes. Although nearly all alliums started out in the Northern Hemisphere, onions, garlic, and their relations have been intrinsic to cuisines worldwide for centuries. They are also considered a "superfood"—full of antioxidants and good for the blood and the immune system.

Growing Tips Alliums share a general preference for loamy, well-drained soil with a neutral pH, even moisture, and full sun, although chives and some garlic varieties will tolerate partial shade, and wild leek (*Allium tricoccum*) requires shady conditions. Keep weeds down with generous applications of mulch—the shallow root systems of alliums can't take much competition. Deer and rodents steer clear of most alliums; slugs are sometimes a problem.

Propagation Either perennials or biennials and often grown as annuals for eating purposes, alliums don't bloom the first season they are planted (plant in fall for next summer's flowers). Bear in mind that you'll get bigger bulbs by carefully removing flowering stalks in the summer. Onions and other alliums that require time to develop a bulb are most commonly grown from sets (small bulbs less than an inch across) and planted either in fall or early spring. You can also purchase starts, young green plants with 6- to 8-inch stems. Plant them out as soon as the soil can be worked in the spring. Several species, like chives, will quickly naturalize into clumps.

Harvesting and Eating Whether or not the plant produces an underground bulb—the part that usually comes to mind when considering onions, shallots, and garlic for the table—the tender young green leaves and whitish stems of almost all alliums (generally referred to as green onions) are also very tasty and may be eaten raw or cooked. The young curling scapes of hardneck garlic are delicious pickled or sautéed. The bulbs of some alliums are so sulfurous (the stink and tear factor) that braising or stewing is necessary to tame them; others, like Vidalia onions, have such a high sugar and water content that they can be eaten out of hand like an apple. The more pungent and less watery the bulb, the better it keeps, however.

Onion | *Allium cepa*

Common onions can be divided into two camps: fresh onions and storing onions. The former are sweet, delicate slicers, usually sold loose; the latter are the denser yellow, white, and purple bulbs sold in mesh bags and best for cooking. Onions depend on both daylight and temperature to form bulbs. Some types (known as long-day onions)

Grow chives (*Allium schoenoprasum*) and herbs like peppermint (*Mentha* × *piperita*) and golden oregano (*Oreganum vulgare* 'Aureum') near the bed's edge for handy harvesting.

are more suited to growing in the north, with its 13- to 16-hour-long summer days, and some (short-day onions) prefer the less varied day length of the south. For this reason, it's worth doing a little extra research before choosing varieties for your garden.

Garlic | *Allium sativum*

There are two main subspecies of garlic: hardneck, or topset, garlic (*Allium sativum* var. *ophioscorodon*) and softneck garlic (*A. sativum* var. *sativum*). Hardneck garlic produces a twisting, snakelike scape up to 24 inches long; the young curling scapes of hardneck garlic varieties, like the popular Rocambole type, are delicious pickled or sautéed. Softneck garlic keeps longer than hardneck and is the type most commonly found in grocery stores (especially cultivars like 'Silverskin'). It rarely sends up a flower stalk, hence its "softneck" moniker, and doesn't take well to cold climates, so avoid softneck garlic in northern zones. Garlic is planted in the fall using cloves from a mature bulb; in mild climates they will grow all winter, but in cold regions they'll go dormant until spring.

Leek | *Allium ampeloprasum* var. *porrum*

Leeks are easy to grow from seed or starts and aren't impatient to be harvested, making them a great allium for beginning gardeners. Plant them in loose, humus rich soil with a regular supply of water and full sun. They can stay in the ground through autumn at least—or you can harvest some early and enjoy their scallion-like flavor.

The hearty green-blue upper leaves of leeks add great ornamental interest to mid-border, with other plants that can support them a little if they start to droop (leeks can reach 2 to 3 feet in height).

Shallot | *Allium cepa* var. *aggregatum*

Shallots, perhaps the most delicately flavored bulbing onions, can transform simple sauces, savory dishes, and vinaigrettes into gourmet fare. Planted in early spring in much the same way as garlic, with cloves just peeking out of the soil, bulbs will multiply to produce between 5 and 10 shallots. Harvest them when the top leaves wilt and start to yellow.

Chives | *Allium schoenoprasum*

Grow chives as a perennial (hardy in Zones 3 to 9) at the front of the bed; they're short (12 to 18 inches), with edible lavender or white pom-pom flowers in summer and evergreen shoots that can be harvested with a snip of the scissors well into winter in warmer zones. They will form clumps if left in the ground year-round and can be propagated by division. 'Forescate' has rosy-pink flowers.

Scallion, Green Onion, Bunching Onion | *Allium fistulosum*

Many are the culinary charms of fresh-cut scallions. Lesser known are the plant's ornamental assets: On second-year plants, this tall allium (18 to 24 inches) bears starry white flowers that liven up the border. 'Santa Claus' has a red stem that adds color to salads.

Ramp, Wild Leek | *Allium tricoccum*

With a flavor that melds garlic and green onion, ramps are one of the earliest greens of the year, excellent in egg dishes, sauteed in butter, and pickled. Ramps are native

to mountainous areas of eastern North America and are not widely grown. Some botanists now advocate their cultivation to help preserve the plant in the wild, which is endangered in some regions. If your garden contains a shady patch that resembles forest floor, try sowing some seeds directly into the soil in late summer and early fall, mulching generously with leaf litter. Lightly harvest the leaves in the spring, leaving the tasty scallion-like bulbs in the ground to naturalize. The foot-tall leaves soon die back, replaced by a flower stalk topped with delicate white blossoms.

Walking Onion | *Allium cepa × proliferum*

This tall perennial (3 feet tall, Zones 3 to 9) is called walking onion for its interesting habit of propagating itself: It forms top-heavy, red-skinned bulbils at the top of its flower stalk, which topple headfirst to the soil to allow the bulbils to take root. The bulbils, an inch or so across, are good sliced in salads or cooked; the oniony leaves are also edible.

Elephant Garlic, Broadleaf Wild Leek
Allium ampeloprasum var. *ampeloprasum*

This bulb-forming leek has long strappy leaves and purple to white flowers on 18- to 24-inch stalks. Snap off the flower heads for bigger bulbs, and harvest when the leaves turn brown. The mild, garlicky-flavored bulbs are wonderful roasted and keep for weeks in a cool dry spot.

Nodding Onion | *Allium cernuum*

Among the prettiest of the edible alliums is the native nodding onion; its 18-inch scape produces a drooping umbel of bell-like white to pinkish flowers. Perennial in Zones 4 to 8, nodding onion can tolerate partial shade, sandy soil, and dry conditions once established. It is easily grown from seed and will spread if not deadheaded. Though nodding onion does not enjoy the same culinary popularity now as it did with Native American tribes and early European settlers, the bulbs and leaves can be used in soups and stews or eaten raw.

Garlic Chives | *Allium tuberosum*

Garlic chives have very attractive fragrant white umbels that bloom above the leaves on stalks 18 to 30 inches tall in late summer. The garlicky leaves and flowers are used extensively in Chinese, Korean, Vietnamese, and Japanese cuisines and are wonderful raw on omelets and salads. Hardy in Zones 3 to 9, garlic chives naturalize readily and can get out of hand; a less aggressive but just as tasty alternative is *Allium ramosum,* fragrant-flowered garlic (Zones 3 to 8), which blooms in early summer.

**1 garlic, 2 leek, 3 shallot, 4 chives, 5 walking onion,
6 garlic chives**

Beets and Chard

Beets and chard have frilly, colorful leaves and stems that add visual zest to the edible landscape. The red-veined foliage of beet greens goes nicely planted near chartreuse lettuce and marigolds; the thick stalks of chard contribute flashes of gold, citrine, and ruby from beneath tall, upright leaves at midborder or in container plantings. Both are variants of *Beta vulgaris* and were first cultivated in the eastern Mediterranean and Middle East. Chard has been grown for its mild-tasting leaves and fleshy stalks since ancient Greek times, and in recent years it's also been bred for beauty. Long considered only a potherb, beet is now mostly grown for its plump, sugary, nutritious root, which may be blood red, pink, white, yellow, or even candy-striped.

Growing Tips Light, sandy, rich soils are ideal for beets and chard. Ample irrigation during dry spells will deter bolting and keep the foliage from turning bitter, as will planting in partial shade (such as near taller plants). Compost and aged manure worked into the soil is good, but be aware that nitrogen-rich soil encourages foliage over root growth.

Propagation After soaking it for a day in water, sow beet seed directly in the bed in early spring, ½-inch deep and 1 inch apart. When the plants are a few inches high, thin to about 4 inches apart (or not, if you're just interested in the foliage). Sow again every few weeks until late summer for steady greens and fall root crops—beetroot can stay in the ground well after frost. Chard seed also benefits from presoaking and can be sown directly in the garden as soon as the soil can be worked; thin seedlings to about 3 inches apart.

Amaranthus tricolor | Joseph's Coat

A goosefoot family (Chenopodiaceae) relative of beets, chard, and spinach, this tropical Asian annual can reach 5 feet tall and 1 to 2 feet wide. It has rather

nondescript flower spikes but spectacular clumps of 5-inch-long red, yellow, and green leaves that taste somewhat like spinach when steamed or sautéed. Start seeds indoors 6 to 8 weeks before the last frost, or outdoors later in the season—it needs warm soil to grow. Joseph's coat prefers full sun and very well-draining soil. To encourage bushy foliage, trim it back when it's about a foot tall.

Beet greens, beetroot 'Chioggia', chard

Beet | *Beta vulgaris*

Both beet greens and beetroot are valued for their earthy, complex flavor and nutritional merits, including vitamins A, C, and numerous Bs, as well as iron, potassium, and fiber. Begin harvesting beet greens for salad when it's time to thin the plants for root development (when the roots are about pencil thick—around 35 days from planting). Cut outer leaves with scissors throughout the season, making sure to leave enough foliage to nourish the roots. Older leaves are tasty lightly sautéed like chard. Beetroot gives the most nutritional punch grated raw in salads, but it's delicious roasted or boiled, peeled, and then glazed in sugar and butter or tossed in a balsamic vinaigrette. Beets are also excellent candidates for pickling, canning, and freezing.

Heirloom 'Bull's Blood' is appealing as a salad green and a root vegetable, and its large, frilly burgundy-red leaves to 18 inches tall are about as ornamental as any foliage out there. The globe-shaped roots, which are dark red shot through with a pinkish bull's-eye pattern, can be harvested at about 60 days. The distinctive red-and-white-striped flesh of 'Chioggia' becomes a bit diffuse with cooking but still stands out.

Chard | *Beta vulgaris* var. *cicla*

Start harvesting outer leaves of chard in four to six weeks from planting. Though it will eventually bolt and decline in warm climates, chard is very cold hardy and can be picked in northern gardens until Thanksgiving, or even later if given protection. It will also grow back if trimmed back entirely to within a couple of inches of the crown. More mature stalks can be tough and are best separated from the green leafy parts, chopped, and cooked separately. Chard is wonderful simply sautéed with garlic and seasoned with lemon juice or tarted up with eggs, cream, Parmesan cheese, pine nuts, and nutmeg to make the classic Sicilian savory. For drama, select cultivars such as 'Bright Lights', 'Ruby Red', and 'Golden Sunrise', whose ruffled dark green leaves stand on rainbow-hued stalks up to 2 feet tall.

Blackberries and Raspberries

Brambles, so called for their tendency to form snarled thickets of prickly canes—the fabled briar patch—are nevertheless worthy elements of the edible landscape when kept in check. Blackberries and raspberries (members of the genus *Rubus*) have been important, if seasonally limited, sources of sweet nutrition for humans since the days of the earliest hunter-gatherers. Wild berry picking along forest edges and roadsides is still a summer tradition, the sweet-tart, sun-warmed little fruits well worth the pokes and scratches. Cultivation for fewer thorns and seeds, longer seasons, larger fruits, and disease resistance has made the backyard garden a less painful, but just as delicious, destination for the latter-day hunter-gatherer.

Growing Tips Bramble fruits are hardy perennials that produce biennial canes. First-year canes (called primocanes) grow vegetatively; second-year canes (floricanes) bloom and fruit, then die. The plants will grow in partial shade but fruit best with full sun, in moist, well-drained average soil with a pH around 6. Mulch, and fertilize occasionally with composted manure. Depending on the species and cultivar, their habit may be erect, trailing, or bushy, with single-stemmed or branching canes. Trellising or supporting the canes with wires or against a fence will make maintenance and harvesting easier. Canes that have produced fruit should be removed at the end of the season, along with any damaged or diseased stems. Most brambles readily spread by suckering, so factor this in when siting your patch and be prepared to do a lot of culling. Air circulation is important to avoid the many diseases raspberries and blackberries are prone to, including *Verticillium* wilt and *Botrytis cinerea* (gray mold). Pick off Japanese beetles, which adore bramble leaves and fruit.

Propagation To avoid inheriting diseases from divisions of old plants, buy bare-root first- or second-year plants and plant them in early spring in the north or in late fall in Zone 6 and southward, dumping in the planting hole some well-rotted manure or compost. Keep new plants well watered. Most blackberries and raspberries are easily propagated by suckers, but some trailing raspberry varieties need to be tip-layered.

Harvesting and Eating Bramble fruits don't travel well and are hard to find and expensive at the market—this alone is reason to grow them. Pick blackberries in late summer when they are shiny, plump, and dark purple-black. The fruit should readily come loose from the calyx; if you need to tug, leave it to ripen another day (or if it's a hot summer morning, try again later that afternoon). Immature blackberries are red and may be confused with raspberries—if it comes off the vine with its core (rasp) intact, it's a blackberry; if it comes off without it, it's a raspberry. Ripe raspberry

Blackberry, raspberry

drupelets practically drop from the plant; if they're overripe they tend to crumble, but even so, you can cook with them.

Of course, tasting is the best test for the first few, then look for the ones that resemble the yummiest testers. The delicate, perfumy flavor of fresh raspberries, especially, is sublime. What you can't eat fresh, you can make into jam, can, or freeze for later use in cobblers, sauces, cordials, and ice cream. If you want to keep the berries' shape when freezing, place them in a single layer on a cookie sheet and freeze them solid before shaking into a freezer bag. Raspberry leaves can be dried and used to make herbal tea.

Blackberry | *Rubus fruticosus*

Blackberry shrubs are generally hardy in Zones 3 to 9, but some cultivars are less cold hardy than others. The canes may grow 7 feet or more; prune the them back to about 3 feet in late winter to encourage lateral branching and keep the fruit within reach. Clusters of small white to pale pink flowers appear in midspring and ripen 40 to 70 days after flowering. 'Black Satin' is a bushy, thornless cultivar to only about 3 feet tall.

Raspberry | *Rubus idaeus*

Raspberries don't tolerate heat as well as blackberries but are hardy in Zones 3 to 8 and usually grow 3 to 6 feet tall; in late winter, prune the cane tips back to live tissue. They take 30 to 50 days to go from clusters of white flowers to ripe fruit, about July. Some types produce a second crop in the fall. The fruits are usually hues of dusky red but may also be purple-black or even yellow. *Rubus idaeus* 'Kiwigold' (Zones 5 to 8) is a yellow-fruited selection that produces two flushes of fruit on the same cane. *Rubus rolfei*, creeping raspberry, is a sun-loving evergreen groundcover that only grows to about 6 inches tall. It has white flowers and produces sparse, tiny but tasty fruit (Zones 6 to 9).

Blueberries

Four-season beauties in the landscape, most *Vaccinium* species also bear highly palatable fruit. These native perennials are a boon for wildlife as well as berry-loving humans, serving bees, butterfly and moth larvae, songbirds, and mammals. Among the hardest-working shrubs in the business, blueberries are grown as crop plants as well as ornamentals. The northern highbush blueberry, *Vaccinium corymbosum*, is the most popular species in cultivation, with selections to suit almost any garden situation. Low-growing *V. angustifolium*, long a favorite of wild berry pickers in rugged, sunny fields in the Northeast and Great Lakes regions, has a large fan base among container and roof gardeners.

Growing Tips For the most fruit and prettiest fall color, plant blueberry shrubs in full sun. They require acidic soil to thrive, ideally around pH 4.5 to 5. A bark or pine straw mulch will help acidify the soil and also keep weeds from competing with the shrub's shallow root system, which appreciates the mulch's moisture-retaining qualities. The large number of cultivars provides a wide range of blooming and fruiting times; depending on your climate and space for growing, you could pick blueberries from early summer almost to frost. Both highbush and lowbush blueberries take several years to produce fruit, but once they do, light pruning in late winter will keep the berries coming. They are both nearly pest free except for birds, which consider the fruit fair game.

Propagation Blueberries can be grown from cuttings, or less reliably, from seed. Nurseries generally sell shrubs as two-year plants, either bare root or in containers. To get the best fruit set, select at least two cultivars of the same species that bloom at the same time.

Black Huckleberry
Gaylussacia baccata

Black huckleberry is native to the eastern half of North America (except Florida) and hardy in Zones 3 to 8. It is a close relative of *Vaccinium*, with a habit and cultural requirements similar to lowbush blueberry. A subshrub in the wild, reaching about 3 feet in height, black huckleberry has shiny leaves dotted with spots of resin and small, bell-shaped pinkish-white flowers. Its late-summer berries are small—about ¼ inch in diameter—and dark reddish purple. In fall, the leaves turn a vibrant coppery red.

Highbush blueberry, lowbush blueberry flowers

Harvesting and Eating Low in calories, loaded with vitamins C and K and manganese, blueberries are high in fiber and have antioxidant properties. Unripe fruits are white to pink-lavender; they are ready to pick when they've turned a dusty dark blue. Highbush blueberries, especially cultivars selected for large berry size, tend to have a high water content that makes them better for eating fresh than for cooking. Try freezing them for a sweet treat on a hot day, or throw them into the blender with yogurt and whatever else you want for a smoothie. The intense sweetness of lowbush blueberries makes them perfect for canning and baking into pies and jam.

Highbush Blueberry | *Vaccinium corymbosum*
Highbush blueberry is tolerant of many garden conditions—full sun to partial shade, wet to somewhat dry, loamy to sandy soils. Most cultivars are hardy in Zones 3 to 7. In the wild, highbush blueberry may grow up to 12 feet tall and wide; most cultivars are about half that size. Popular cultivars include 'Patriot', 'Bluecrop', and 'Elliot'; 'Sharpblue', and 'Jubilee' can tolerate more heat than the straight species (hardy to Zone 9 at least).

Lowbush Blueberry | *Vaccinium angustifolium*
Lowbush blueberry is an open, twiggy subshrub that grows only 6 inches to 2 feet tall and wide. The showy white urn-shaped flowers produce small blue-black fruits that are sweeter and more intensely flavored than highbush blueberries. Though hardy far into the icy north (Zones 2 to 6) and low maintenance, it needs full sun and good drainage to perform well. There are relatively few cultivars of lowbush blueberry, but there are a good many "half-high" crosses with *Vaccinium corymbosum*, such as 'Top Hat', which bears fruit without a pollinator. They grow to between 2 and 4 feet tall and are suitable for containers.

Brassicas

Though grown for centuries as staple crops with little consideration for their decorative value, many brassicas nevertheless offer lovely color and structural drama to borders and container gardens. Selections of *Brassica oleracea*— including kale, collards, cauliflower, broccoli, kohlrabi, brussels sprouts, and cabbage—are extremely diverse and difficult to classify due to millennia of selection and interbreeding. Some form their leaves in a tightly packed head; others have been bred to grow them loosely. A few, such as broccoli and cauliflower, have been cultivated for their immature inflorescences, and kohlrabi is grown for its bulbous stem rather than its leaves.

Growing Tips Brassicas are heavy feeders and need well-draining, organically rich soil to access nitrogen and micronutrients like iron. Unlike many other vegetables, brassicas grow best in soils with near neutral pH (around 6 to 7); add lime if necessary. Plant them in full sun and water regularly to avoid wilting and cracking of heading varieties. Brassicas prefer the cool growing conditions of spring and fall and may bolt (send up a flower stalk) in hot weather. Keep a lookout for cabbage butterfly caterpillars, aphids, and flea beetles and fungal diseases. Pick off the caterpillars; hose off the insects; and cut down on disease with good air circulation, weeding, and by planting brassicas in different plots from year to year. To avoid *Fusarium* wilt in warm climates, select resistant cultivars.

Propagation Though treated as annuals for eating purposes, most brassicas are biennials or even perennials. For early-spring planting, start seeds five to seven weeks before the last frost; seedlings tolerate cool spring weather and can be hardened off for transplanting as soon as they're 4 to 6 inches high. Plant seeds for fall and winter harvest in late June or July.

Harvesting and Eating Collards and kales can be harvested throughout the season as long as you pick only outer leaves and leave the inner ones. Broccoli can also regrow after the heads are cut if the leaf crowns are left intact. Some cauliflower cultivars need to be "blanched"—outer leaves pulled up and tied over the developing head—to keep the head pure white. In the Northeast, collards, kale, brussels sprouts, and cabbage can be picked until snow flies, often until Thanksgiving or later if covered. The flavor of most brassicas improves with a little frost, making them ideal for holding in the garden as long as possible.

All brassicas are high in vitamins and minerals, including the various Bs, C, K, A, potassium, and dietary fiber, plus carotinoids and other nutrients with antioxidant and immune-boosting properties. Steaming, lightly stir-frying, or not cooking at all are the best preparations for retaining the most nutrients in brassicas, especially

The beautiful prehistoric-looking Tuscan kale (*Brassica oleracea* 'Lacinato'), also known as dinosaur kale for its pebbly green-black leaves, adds a bold vertical accent to the garden.

those credited with preventing cancer. These same methods also cut down on the production of the sulfurous "cabbagy" smell released with boiling. The large, robust leaves of most cabbages, collards, and kales makes it necessary to shred or slice and sometimes devein them before eating, but this same toughness is what makes cabbage wonderful for wrapping other foods for steaming and braising.

Broccoli | *Brassica oleracea* var. *italica*
There are two main types of broccoli: smaller, early-growing cultivars like 'Green Comet' that produce one main central head in early summer, and larger, later varieties like 'De Cicco', an Italian heirloom, that send up many side shoots after the central head is cut, great for harvesting throughout the season. The regenerating broccolis require more space than earlier ones. Harvest all broccoli when buds are fully developed but before they loosen and begin to flower.

Cauliflower, Romanesco | *Brassica oleracea* var. *botrytis*
Like cabbages and broccoli, cauliflower can grow to more than 2 feet tall and wide and become a little blousy with maturity; transplant the seedlings about 18 to 24 inches apart to keep them from shading out other plants. Try an orange- or purple-headed cultivar for extra color. Not commonly seen in gardens is one of the most spectacular brassica forms, the romanesco cauliflower (or broccoli, depending on

whom you ask). A marvel of natural fractals, its head of pointy chartreuse spirals resembles an exotic seashell; 'Veronica' develops a chartreuse head (curd) in cool climates; in warm conditions, it may be creamy white with pinkish hues. It is best eaten raw.

Cabbage | *Brassica oleracea* var. *capitata*

Planted in rows along the sides of the border, placed as focal points front and center, or tucked among the tomatoes in a container, the glaucous green globes, ruby-red balls, and crinkly, savoyed heads of cabbages make them the kings of the ornamental vegetable garden. Some varieties mature very quickly, making them excellent for summer menus; others grow more slowly, producing larger, more tightly packed heads that store well. Spend some time with your seed catalogs to choose the right varieties for your needs.

The flavor and texture of the green-headed 'Tendersweet', as its name implies, make it perfect for coleslaw. 'Mammoth Red' produces large, purple heads that weigh up to seven pounds. 'Copenhagen Market' is a Danish heirloom ideal for smaller gardens.

Brussels Sprouts | *Brassica oleracea* (Gemmifera group)

Knobby-stemmed brussels sprouts add a note of vaguely tropical whimsy to beds and pots. The plants take up quite a bit of space, needing at least 18 to 24 inches

Mustard Greens | *Brassica juncea*

A fast-growing cool-weather green, mustard can be sown as soon as the ground can be worked for a nutritious spring tonic. Pick the young leaves to add zest to salads before their tangy bite gets too strong and must be tamed by cooking. Once the weather warms, give up on harvesting and let it send up its 2-foot stalk covered

with pretty yellow flowers. Plant another crop near the end of summer for another flush of greens. Among the most decorative cultivars are 'Osaka Purple', which has round, purple-tinged leaves with white veins; 'Red Giant', with small savoyed burgundy leaves with light green veins; and 'Southern Giant Curled', with 18- to 24-inch green, frilly leaves that are edged with yellow at harvest time.

between plants in rows and beds. The sprouts are slow growing, up to 120 days from planting. Snap off leaves from the bottom as stalks grow, and be sure the plants receive adequate water and mulch throughout the summer. 'Long Island' is a high-producing compact variety reaching 2 feet high; 'Red Bull' is a 3-foot stunner, with red foliage and red sprouts that maintain their color after cooking.

Kale | *Brassica oleracea* var. *sabellica*
Collards | *Brassica oleracea* var. *acephala*

Kales (and collards, too) work especially well in the edible landscape; at the back and center of the border, tall, upright cultivars set off flowers and the foliage of other plants. More compact kale varieties, like the colorful ornamental hybrids, make attractive edgings, especially in formal beds. Kales developed for the ornamental trade are perfectly edible; just be sure to grow your own or buy seedlings from organic growers to assure that they have not been treated with insecticides or other chemicals. Tuscan or "dinosaur" kale (*Brassica oleracea* 'Lacinato' and other cultivars) is a popular 2-foot-tall plant with striking deep green, wrinkled leaves 2 to 3 inches wide and 10 inches long.

Kohlrabi | *Brassica oleracea* var. *gongylodes*

With its bulbous stem and vertical turnip-like foliage, kohlrabi is an amusing sight in the garden. It is usually harvested at baseball size or smaller, when its crunchy, sweet flesh is best eaten raw, but the giant 'Superschmelz' can grow into a yellow volleyball before becoming too woody to eat. 'Kolibri', with its vibrant purple globe and stems, adds lots of ground-level color to beds.

1 romanesco, 2 cauliflower, 3 savoy cabbage,
4 brussels sprouts, 5 Tuscan kale, 6 kohlrabi

Cardoon and Globe Artichoke

Native to Mediterranean Europe and North Africa, cardoons and globe artichokes have been gourmet vegetables at least since the time of ancient Greece. Cardoons (*Cynara cardunculus*), widely grown in European potagers for their mild-flavored fleshy stems, are less well known to American palates than artichokes, the delectible immature flower buds of the globe artichoke, thought to be a cultivated descendant of *C. cardunculus*. These architecturally striking plants produce handsome, deeply serrated gray-green leaves on robust arching stalks; attractive thistlelike purple flowers surrounded by spiky green bracts appear in late summer. The vase-shaped plants can reach 3 to 6 feet tall and 2 to 3 feet wide. Place them singly or in small, well-spaced groupings as focal points in the border or in a container planting.

Growing Tips *Cynara* plants prefer rich, deep, well-drained moist soil that is slightly acidic to neutral, with an occasional application of nitrogen-rich fertilizer such as fish emulsion. They grow best in full sun. Wear gardening gloves when handling the plants to avoid painful pricks from the spiky leaves and bracts. If aphids—one of the plants' few pests—attack, knock them off with a blast from the hose. In Zones 7 to 11, cardoons and globe artichokes will grow for four to five years before declining. To overwinter the plant in cooler climates, cut it back to the ground after the first frost, mulch heavily, and cover it with clear plastic or an overturned pot, or consider digging up the deep-growing roots and storing them until spring.

In cool regions where *Cynara* is unlikely to escape cultivation, the fluffy-looking flower heads may be left on the plants for winter interest; otherwise take care to trim off the heads before their seeds can spread. Brought to the Americas with European exploration, by the time of Charles Darwin's *Beagle* voyage, *Cynara* (most likely globe artichokes reverted to a wild form) could be found growing thickly in parts of Argentina, where even then it was considered a noxious weed—as it is today in parts of the North American west.

Propagation In cool climates, start both cardoons and globe artichoke seeds four to eight weeks before the last frost. Unless you are planting one of the newer, more hardy cultivars bred to produce buds in one growing season, you can vernalize the plants to get a first-year harvest of chokes: After the indoor-planted seedlings sprout, set them outdoors for a few weeks while the weather is still very cool, in March and April (bringing them in or otherwise protecting them from freezing temperatures). Wait to transplant them outdoors until the soil is reliably warm (about 75°F). You can also transplant divisions or root cuttings of older plants after all danger of frost is past.

Globe artichoke, cardoon

Cardoon | *Cynara cardunculus*

The edible leaf ribs of cardoons can be bitter if not blanched several weeks before harvest: Gather up the leaves from the plant base and wrap them loosely in a spiral of twine, then shield the exposed stalks from the sun with a layer of craft paper or burlap. The leaf stalks are ready to cut when the leaves and stems have turned a light yellow or white (about 120 to 150 days after planting). Cardoons, which have a mild artichoke flavor, may be frozen or canned, but they are best eaten soon after harvesting, served raw in vinaigrettes, sautéed or steamed with butter, and gratinée. The flowers may also be used as a vegetarian rennet substitute in cheese making. 'Gobbo di Nizza' is an Italian cultivar with white stems. 'Porto Spineless', as its name suggests, is gentler on gardeners' hands.

Globe Artichoke | *Cynara cardunculus* (Scolymus group)

Use sharp pruners to harvest the swollen globe artichoke buds just before they bloom (about 85 days after planting out), when the outer bracts begin to open but before the purple flower itself appears. Trim the tough, spiny outer bracts and remove the fibrous prebloom flower (the choke), leaving the "heart" and fleshy inner bracts. They are delicious trimmed and steamed, roasted, or deep-fried whole and served with lemon aioli. Globe artichokes can also be stuffed and baked and pickled for use in salads and dips. In the unlikely event that your harvest is not immediately feasted upon, artichokes can be blanched and frozen.

The cultivar 'Imperial Star' produces small but tasty artichokes in one season (85 to 105 days) and can thus be grown as an annual. 'Violetto' is an heirloom cultivar with lovely purple, slightly pointed artichokes (which unfortunately turn green after a few minutes of cooking); it is usually grown as a second-year crop. 'Green Globe' produces artichokes 3 to 4 inches in diameter its second year, given winter protection.

Chile Peppers

Chile peppers have been cultivated for food and medicine for almost as long as Central and South America have been populated. Chiles' decorative value derives from the bushy dark green to purple foliage and vivid shiny fruits, which usually start out green or purplish brown and ripen to bright hues of yellow, orange, or red and vary wildly in shape and size. Flowers of white, yellow, or shades of purple appear early and are pollinated by insects, mostly bees, before forming fruits, which may be upward facing or drooping, single or clustered. Cultivars developed specifically for their striking peppers are usually short and lush, perfect for the front of the border and containers.

Growing Tips A perennial in tropical regions, peppers are generally considered annuals in North American gardens. Most chile peppers prefer full sun and sandy, rich soil with a pH of 5.5 to 6.5, good drainage, and consistent moisture. Plant where no other members of the Solanaceae (tomato and potato family) have recently grown, since the family shares many diseases. Mulch with straw, and keep a lookout for aphids. Peppers like warm weather with regular watering. Potted ornamentals can be brought inside to extend the season.

Propagation There are more than a score of *Capiscum* species, but only five are widely cultivated, and the best-known forms are members of *C. annuum* or *C. chinense*. Many chile cultivars are available as starts, ready to transplant as soon as you buy them, but the seed catalogs are still the place to go for hundreds of rare and unusual ornamental peppers. Some varieties are ready to harvest in just over two months, but others can take 120 days or more to mature, so in many U.S. regions, pepper seeds must be started indoors or in a cold frame in early spring. Plant seeds in peat pots eight weeks before the last frost; keep in a warm, well-lit spot and repot if necessary before planting out only when the soil is reliably warm (65°F).

Harvesting and Eating Pick your first crop when the chiles are still somewhat immature (usually this means green), which will stimulate more blooming and fruiting for later in the season. Cut the fruit from the stems with a knife or clippers, and wear gloves (capsaicin, the active compound in chiles, can be

More About Chile Peppers

Edible peppers are so varied they could occupy an entire book—so we wrote one! To learn more about growing and harvesting more than 50 varieties of chile peppers, see the BBG handbook *Chile Peppers: Hot Tips and Tasty Picks for Gardeners and Gourmets* (bbg.org/handbooks).

Ornamental pepper 'Black Pearl', habanero, cayenne

irritating to the skin). Some peppers, such as sweet bells and cubanelles, have little or no heat value (as measured from mild to beyond fiery on the Scoville scale) and are widely eaten raw in salads and crudités, fried, or stuffed and baked. On up the heat scale, chiles are used worldwide fresh, pickled, smoked, or dried and added in various amounts to condiments, salsas, chili, stir-fries, curries, grilled meats—anything that needs spicing up.

Bell, Hungarian, Ancho, Jalapeño, Serrano, etc. | *Capsicum annuum*

This species offers the most variety in size, shape, and heat among chiles. Sweet softball-size bell peppers (now in green, yellow, orange, red, and purple) and mild banana-shaped peppers like 'Hungarian Yellow Wax' are popular vegetable garden plants and tend to grow bigger than ornamentals (1 to 4 feet tall and wide). Mildly hot 'Holy Mole' grows to 3 feet tall and has long, tapered green to chocolate-hued peppers to 9 inches long. 'Ancho 101', despite its modern-sounding name, has been cultivated for thousands of years. Fresh green anchos—called poblanos—grow on 3-foot, spreading plants and are prized for making chiles rellenos. For tight spaces, borders, or containers, try the wildly colorful (and hot) ornamental pepper 'Black Pearl', a prizewinning black-leafed beauty about 1 foot high and wide with clusters of round fruits that mature from purple-black to scarlet.

Scotch Bonnet, Datil, Habanero, etc. | *Capsicum chinense*

Capsicum chinense includes some of the hottest peppers in the world. Plants grow 1 to 3 feet tall and have large, wrinkly leaves and often rather shriveled-looking small, lantern-shaped fruit. 'Chocolate Habanero' has 2-inch fruits maturing from green to rich brown to red; near the top of the Scoville scale, it is used like Scotch bonnet to make Caribbean jerk sauce.

Cucurbits

Native to the tropics of Asia, Africa, and the Americas, melons, cucumbers, and squashes are among the earliest cultivated plants. These (mostly) annual vines also serve well as ornamentals: Except for the heaviest pumpkins and squashes, cucurbits (members of the Cucurbitaceae) can be trained on trellises and tuteurs for vertical drama, the spiraling tendrils along the stems arching out to clasp whatever they touch, the large, palmately lobed emerald leaves growing progressively smaller toward the stem tips. Large orange, yellow, or pale cream flowers bloom all summer, their numbers making up for their one-day existence.

Growing Tips Cucurbits rely on warm weather and regular but not excessive watering. If drainage is not superb, plant cucurbits in mounds (this also makes weeding and bug searching a little easier). Plant them in full sun in rich, slightly acidic soil, and mulch with compost or straw. Cucumbers, miniature pumpkins and melons, and summer squash intended for early harvest may be trellised; others, such as standard pumpkins, hubbards, and watermelons, may be grown unsupported, with trailing stems snaking among taller plants that won't be smothered by the large shady foliage.

Propagation Cucurbits require warm soil to germinate, and many need a long growing season for fruit to mature (up to three or four months); in cooler climates, plant seeds indoors, harden off after the last frost, and transplant when the soil is at least 60°F. In regions with long growing seasons, seeds can be sown directly; some gardeners plant cucurbits in groups of three or four on low hills or mounds of soil and later remove all but the strongest seedling. Garden centers also offer nursery-grown starts at the proper time for planting out.

Most cucurbits are monoecious, with both male and female flowers on the same plant; the male flowers appear first, followed by female blossoms (usually recognizable by the small bulbous shape of the base). Bees are the best pollinators for cucurbits. Pick off pests like disease-carrying cucumber beetles, and avoid planting cucurbits in the same spot from year to year to avoid blossom-end rot and *Fusarium* and bacterial wilts.

Harvesting and Eating The generous yield and relatively poor keeping ability of summer squashes have led to a lot of creativity in the kitchen: They are eaten raw or sautéed, stuffed and baked, and grated for use in savory or sweet puddings and breads; blossoms are delicious sautéed or batter-dipped and fried. Longer-keeping winter types, which can remain in the garden until well after the foliage has been frostbitten, are great baked (sans seeds and fibrous pith) with butter and maple syrup;

The rambling, groundcovering habit of squash and melon plants can be used as a lovely living mulch to smother weeds and keep other plants' roots cool and moist.

the high-fiber, beta-carotene-rich flesh can be pureed for use in desserts and soups or cooked in chunks with stews, and their seeds can be roasted as a snack. Melons like cantaloupes, casabas, and honeydews are valued for their juicy sweetness and eaten raw: Harvest when the skin color has lost its greenness and become pale golden. Try sniffing the fruit for a perfumy melon scent that signals ripeness; if it smells green or has no odor at all, let it stay on the vine a few more days. Watermelon is ready to pick when you hear a resonant, low response to a thump with your finger.

Summer Squashes | *Cucurbita pepo*

Zucchini, crookneck, pattypan, and other summer squash (varieties best harvested and eaten immature, before the skins harden), are among the easiest plants for first-time gardeners to grow, and they start producing fruits for the table only 40 to 60 days from planting. They can be trained to grow vertically on a trellis as long as the fruits are picked before their weight pulls down the vine. 'Cocozelle' and 'Black Beauty' zucchini are both compact, bushy, steady producers—great choices for small gardens; 'Eight Ball' has baseball-size dark green fruits. The heirloom 'Pattison Panache Verte et Blanc' yields light green scalloped pattypan squash after 60 days (or earlier for pickling-size pattypans); and 'Summer Crookneck' will keep you stocked with bumpy-skinned schoolbus-yellow squash until frost.

Winter Squashes | *Cucurbita maxima, C. pepo*, and *C. moschata*

Acorn, butternut, hubbard, pumpkin, and other winter squash are wildly variable and bring substantial ornamental interest to borders, terraces, and even lawns. They may be smooth, broadly ribbed, or warty and take the shape of jugs, pears, and turbans in hues of orange, variegated green, or dusty blue-gray—the bigger and odder looking, the more fun they are to grow. Winter squashes are left on the vine until their skins have hardened and the seeds have matured. To avoid rot, keep a layer of light mulch like hay beneath the growing fruit. Make sure two inches of stem are left on the squash before storing it in a cool, dry place. *Cucurbita pepo* 'Gill's Golden Pippin' produces bright yellow acorn squash (95 days); tiny white-skinned pumpkin 'Baby Boo' is great for kids' gardens and containers (95 days); *C. maxima* 'Marina di Chioggia' (105 days) is a large, pebbly gray-green turban-shaped squash that is delicious baked.

Cucumber | *Cucumis sativus*

Cucumbers appreciate well-amended, cool soil (with full sun up top) and regular watering—over- or underwatering can both result in bitter fruits. Cucumbers are refreshing in salads or as crudités, but they are most famous for the many ways they can be preserved as pickles—sweet, sour, or salty, sliced, slivered, or whole. They can also be sautéed or baked with butter, lemon juice, and herbs. There are bushels of cucumber cultivars to choose from, falling into two rough categories: slicers, delicious eaten fresh; and picklers, which mature early and can be eaten raw or pickled.

Bitter Melon | *Momordica charantia*

The fruit of bitter melon is popular in Asian cuisines, but it's an acquired taste; if it doesn't agree with your palate, grow it on a trellis as an ornamental like gourds,

which are inedible but well worth growing for their crazy shapes and colors. If left on the vine to ripen, bitter melons turn vivid yellow-orange, split open, and curl back to reveal large, bright red seeds. Start seeds indoors six weeks before the last frost (first soak and then gently crack the seed coats before planting), and transplant outside once the soil is at least 60°F. The tapering, deeply ridged fruits are usually harvested for eating when they are still green and immature.

'Crystal Apple' yields a round, pale yellow cuke, a sweet slicer. 'Parisian Pickling' is a dark-green, bumpy-skinned heirloom, used for tiny cornichon pickles or for eating raw if left to grow a bit bigger.

Melons | *Cucumis melo*

Warm-weather-loving sweet melons like cantaloupe and honeydew are easy to grow in well-draining rich, loamy soil in full sun and usually yield ripe fruit in 65 to 100 days, depending on the variety. For the ornamental garden, try a compact-growing cultivar like 'Minnesota Midget', with sweet golden-yellow fruit small enough to be supported on a trellis. They're ready for the breakfast or dessert table when they drop off the vine by themselves or slip easily from the stem when picked. Casabas, which thrive in hot, nonhumid conditions, need a long growing season. The cultivar 'Golden Beauty' (110 days) has firm white flesh and a yellow, thick skin that makes it a good keeper.

Watermelon | *Citrullus lanatus*

Most watermelon cultivars require an investment of time—about 110 days from seed to ripe fruit—but given a warm, sunny spot, rich soil, and regular watering, they will produce two or three juicy fruits per vine. Look for cultivars to suit your climate and space—short-season ripeners for northern gardens and compact forms for small plots. There's also a lot of variety in shape, size, and color: 'Golden Midget' grows to a petite, three-pound ball with yellow skin and sweet salmon-pink flesh in about 70 days; 'Cream of Saskatchewan' produces green-striped round fruits with crisp, white flesh in 85 days. The round to oblong heirloom 'Moon and Stars' grows large—to 50 pounds if growing conditions are perfect (100 days) and is deep green splotched with dark yellow; it has red flesh, but there is also a yellow-fleshed strain.

1 zucchini, 2 yellow squash, 3 cucumber, 4 cucumber,
5 muskmelon, 6 watermelon

Fruit Trees

The majority of the fruit trees grown in North American gardens are members of the rose family (Rosaceae) and include, among many others, apple, cherry, peach, pear, and plum. The native habitats of these deciduous trees—temperate regions of central to western Asia and the Caucasus—coincided with those of early human farmers. Their palatable, nutritious, and portable fruit ensured dissemination along ancient trade routes and intensive breeding, which have yielded thousands of cultivated varieties. As if showy, fragrant spring blossoms and delicious, attractive fruits weren't reason enough to feature these trees in the edible garden, their versatility in size and habit—standard, dwarf, spreading, columnar, espaliered—merit an important architectural role in the landscape.

Growing Tips The best soil for most rose family trees is deep, loamy to sandy, and well drained, with a pH of 5.5 to 7. Most of these trees are hardy in Zones 5 through 8 (with new cultivars pushing both ends of the tolerance spectrum). All require full sun for good fruit production. Planting on a slight slope helps with drainage and protects early blooms against damage from wind and low-lying frost pockets. In cooler climates, nearby heat-holding walls and hardscape will also protect fruit trees.

To get good fruit set, most of these trees need pollination partners (usually a different cultivar of the same species with an overlapping bloom time), so plan on planting at least two of each type of fruit tree. Rose family trees are prone to similar diseases and pests, including fire blight, scab, and codling moths (apples and pears). Consult your local Cooperative Extension about the hardiest, most disease-resistant cultivars for your area as well as pest management practices. Plant young trees when they are dormant in holes three or four times the diameter of the root ball and just deep enough to fit the roots after all damaged tips have been pruned off. Fill in the hole with the original soil, making sure the graft remains about 2 inches above the soil and the trunk is clear of mulch. As a general rule, prune back new saplings by a third or so, and then let them grow a few seasons before pruning for shape and size—but it's worth researching each tree individually for when and how to prune, fertilize, etc. Keep saplings well watered until they are established; mulch with compost to retain moisture and deter weeds.

Propagation Rose family fruit trees are usually sold as one- or two-year-old nursery-grown saplings from grafted rootstock, since seed-grown trees rarely grow true. Instead, scions (shoots with buds) from trees with desirable traits—say, nice fruit flavor or particular disease resistance—are grafted to rootstock with other desirable traits, such as cold hardiness or dwarfing habit.

Harvesting and Eating It may take five years or more to reap the first fruits of your trees, but it will be worth the wait for that first bite fresh off the branch. To

A peach tree grows in Brooklyn as well as in a country orchard given enough sun and water; a nearby heat-absorbing wall boosts its winter hardiness.

dessert lovers, the very words "cherry," "plum," and "peach" conjure all manner of pastries, pies, sauces, and jams, but their culinary uses go far beyond sweet treats and fruity salads. Brandy, or eau-de-vie, is distilled from them. Sautéed or stewed, they complement roasted and grilled meats, especially game. In addition to their out-of-hand edibility, they are also easily dried, canned, and frozen. Plums are also eaten as pickles and salted prunes.

In addition to the trees described below, other bearers of edible fruit in the rose family include apricot, quince, loquat, medlar, and almond trees. Hybrids between plums, apricots, peaches, and other stone fruits, variously grouped as pluots or apriums, have also been developed in recent years.

Apple | *Malus domestica*

Depending on the rootstock, apple trees can grow anywhere from 3 or 4 feet tall and 1 foot wide to 30 feet tall and 20 feet wide. They may be grown as shade trees, pruned to stay low and compact, or trained to grow flat along a wall as an espalier. Apple blossoms are usually white with a pink tint and appear in early to late spring, depending on the climate and apple variety. Though there aren't nearly as many cultivars today as there were even 100 years ago, careful breeding in recent years has produced trees with delicious fruit and habits suitable for every garden space. For example, 'Sentinel' was selected for its columnar, multispurred habit, making it great for containers, borders, and fencerows. Apples are ready to pick when they look and taste ready—juicy and pleasant, whether tart or sweet. The flesh should be creamy or white, not greenish, with black seeds. Pick them as carefully as possible to avoid pulling off next year's fruiting spur. Store unblemished "keeper" apples in a very cool, humid place away from other vegetables and fruits. Eat or make sauce and apple butter with the rest.

Peach | *Prunus persica*

Unlike others in this family, peaches are self-pollinating. Pink flowers in spring produce peaches that ripen from midsummer to early fall, depending on the cultivar; they are not very cold hardy and need a protected spot in regions that get colder than −10°F in winter. Standard peach trees may be 20 feet tall, but dwarf and semidwarf cultivars are only about half that or less. Peaches take well to pruning and can be kept small for containers that way. They can also be espaliered. Peaches need to ripen on the tree; a ripe peach has no traces of green but rather is yellowish with a pinkish blush and is firm-fleshed but easily twists off the branch. They will keep for a while in a cool spot, but if they are bruised—easy to do—they need to be eaten, frozen, or canned as soon as possible.

Pear | *Pyrus communis*

Among the earliest flowers to appear in the spring, pear blossoms are white, mildly fragrant, and usually profuse. Trees can be used for shade, pruned to live in containers, or espaliered. Once clusters of new fruits appear on the branches, cull them to

Shadbush, Allegheny Serviceberry | *Amelanchier laevis*

On this shrubby North American native tree, early-spring clusters of long-petaled white flowers give way to small red berrylike fruit that ripen to purplish blue in

 midsummer if the birds don't eat them all first. Bright orange to red fall foliage and striped gray bark give it multiseasonal appeal in gardens from Zones 4 to 9. It grows in the wild along forest edges and can tolerate dappled shade. Shadbush can be pruned to be single-stemmed or multibranched, and its tendency to sucker makes it a good candidate for hedge pruning. Shadbush is best propagated by layering sucker cuttings. Use the fruit for jams and cobblers and in muffins.

one pear per cluster to get a single great pear rather than several gnarly small ones whose combined weight might also break the branch. Pears need to be carefully picked before they are fully ripe or they become brown at the core and mealy. Store unripe pears at as close to 32°F as possible; at room temperature they will ripen within a week or so of being picked.

Plum | *Prunus domestica*

Through long cultivation, plums are widely varied, growing from 8 to over 20 feet tall, with white flowers and fruit that may be green, yellow, red, or purple-black and anywhere from the size of a cherry to a baseball. Depending on the cultivar, the habit may be upright and pyramidal or spreading, like a peach tree. Most require pollinating partners of a different cultivar, but some are self-pollinating. Harvest the fruit when they are slightly soft but not mushy, with sweet, juicy flesh offset by the slightly astringent skin; twist slightly to detach from the stem. Most cooking and drying plums are derived from the European species *Prunus domestica*; cultivars of the Asian *P. salicina* are considered the best for eating fresh.

Sweet Cherry | *Prunus avium*

After its delicate white flowers fade in spring, small dark red sweet cherries form in clusters, ready to pick in midsummer. (Like apples, cherries are ready to pick when they look and taste ripe; try to retain the stem when picking.) Though the species can grow to be very large in the wild, up to 60 feet tall, most cultivars are sold on dwarf or semidwarf rootstock, fine for the garden landscape. As with all rose family fruit trees, disease and insects are issues, but birds are the biggest threat to cherry crops. Check with your local Extension office about preventive measures like bird netting. Some sweet cherry cultivars, like 'Stella', are self-pollinating, but others require a cross-pollinator, so you'll need to do your research. Sweet cherries are generally considered best for fresh eating and sour (*Prunus cerasus*) best for cooking.

1 apple, 2 plum, 3 apple, 4 cherry, 5 pear, 6 peach

Herbs of the Carrot Family

Most herbs grown and used by cooks in North America are in one of two globally distributed plant families: carrot (including cilantro, fennel, parsley, and dill) or mint (including thyme, oregano, sage, and rosemary). Herbs of the carrot family (Apiaceae) share bright green, ferny foliage and graceful, fountainlike silhouettes of varying heights. Their flowers are usually white, pink, or yellow umbels on long, straight stalks that attract butterflies and bees. Their decorative, flavorful foliage and seeds are key components in fresh, cooked, and pickled foods around the world. Although many are tender perennials or biennials, for culinary uses they are often grown as annuals.

Growing Tips Moist, well-drained average soil and full sun to partial shade are optimal conditions for most carrot-family herbs. Mulch with hay or compost to keep the ground moist and weeds controlled. In warmer climates, most of these herbs appreciate protection from hot afternoon sun; cilantro in particular prefers cool conditions. The plants decline after setting seed, so to keep them producing aromatic foliage on more branches, snip off bloom stalks as they emerge. Planting new seeds every few weeks over the summer (or at least once toward the end of summer) assures a steady supply of fresh herbs until frost.

Propagation Before planting—either indoors a few weeks before last frost or outdoors when the soil is reliably 50°F—presoak the seeds of carrot-family herbs to aid germination. Plant the seeds about ¼ inch deep. When they are about 2 inches tall, plant out seedlings and thin direct-sown plants: Set cilantro plants close together; parsley and chervil 10 inches apart; fennel about a foot apart. All form taproots and grow best in deep, loose soil; don't move them.

Harvesting and Eating For first harvest, trim plants back to their second or third full set of leaves to encourage fuller branching and foliage. Cutting at least once a month during the growing season (in midmorning, as soon as the dew has dried from the leaves) will keep you well supplied with fresh herbs. Let the herbs bloom toward the end of the season to enjoy their edible flowers and seeds. Harvest seeds for drying just as they begin to brown on the stem. At frost time, harvest and freeze the leaves to retain the most flavor. Fennel, lovage, and parsley may be left to overwinter in permanent beds.

Chervil | *Anthriscus cerefolium*

Chervil can be one of the most beautiful plants in the garden, each clump a mass of fernlike foliage, with tiny white or pinkish-lavender flowers on stalks floating just above the leaves. It grows best with some protection from the hottest part of the day and may reach 1½ feet tall. Commonly found in French kitchens as a key component

The billowy, lacy foliage of umbel herbs like fennel (*Foeniculum vulgare* subsp. *vulgare*) combine with asparagus (*Asparagus officinalis*) to blur the edges of traditional garden rows.

of *fines herbes* blends, chervil is best used fresh, adding a delicate anise flavor to salads, beans, egg dishes, and cream sauces.

Cilantro, Coriander | *Coriandrum sativum*

Cilantro grows 1 to 2 feet tall and wide has light green foliage, with flat, broadly lobed leaves at its base and thinly cut, feathery leaves toward the top of the plant as it forms bloom stalks. A staple flavoring in the cuisines of Asia, India, Mexico, and South America, cilantro adds bright lemony accents to raw and cooked foods alike. Snip the leaves and tender stems until the plant begins to flower, then shift your focus to seeds, which can be dried and ground for use in curries, cookies, and poultry dishes. A slow-bolting cultivar is 'Calypso', which produces superior foliage when periodically snipped back.

Cumin | *Cuminum cyminum*

Ground and whole cumin seeds are used in any number of cuisines worldwide, most notably those of the Mediterranean and Middle East, where the plant originated, as well as Latin America. Growing cumin in North American gardens cooler than Zones 8 to 10 can be a bit of a challenge, as it requires three to four months of summer temperatures, but plants can be started indoors and transplanted in warm weather once

they have at least two sets of true leaves. Cumin reaches 1 to 2 feet in height, with white or pale pink flowers and feathery pinnate foliage. Though mostly grown for its seeds, which are ready to harvest when they crack between your fingers, cumin's fine green leaves are also good sprinkled on salads.

Dill | *Anethum graveolens*

With its large, fragrant yellow flowers and threadlike blue-green foliage on long, 3- to 5-foot-tall stems, dill adds stately elegance to borders and containers. Butterflies, bees, and other beneficial insects will find it quite attractive too. The leaves, called dill weed in culinary parlance to distinguish it from the seeds, are used in fish, egg, and potato dishes, especially in northern European cuisines. The seeds are used in breads, cheese, and cabbage dishes. Jars of pickles are often adorned with sprigs of dill, flower and all. The cultivar 'Bouquet' is excellent for seed harvesting; 'Fernleaf' is a compact selection that reaches 18 inches high, perfect as a container plant.

Fennel | *Foeniculum vulgare*

Fennel—especially its bronze cultivars—is a common backdrop in ornamental borders; it grows 3 to 7 feet tall, with finely cut anise-scented foliage and yellow-flowered umbels (usually in the second year). The plumy purplish-brown foliage of 'Purpureum', bronze fennel, makes it a highly popular decorative cultivar. The leaves and seeds of both common and bronze fennel are used in cooking, imparting a licorice flavor to potato salad and grilled fish. Bulb fennel (*Foeniculum vulgare* subsp. *vulgare*, Azoricum group) is grown for its bulbous stem, which has a delicate anise flavor and is served raw in salads or cooked as a vegetable.

Lovage | *Levisticum officinale*

Lovely at the back of the border, lovage is a robust hardy perennial herb (Zones 3 to 8) that grows 3 to 6 feet tall and 2 feet wide, with shiny bright green

1 chervil, 2 coriander, 3 cumin, 4 dill, 5 dill, 6 fennel

leaves and roundish umbels of yellow-green flowers. The leaves, which have a sharp celery-like flavor, can be eaten raw in salads or cooked in soups and stews; dried lovage seeds are used to spice dressings, breads, and soups.

Parsley | *Petroselinum crispum*

Parsley looks very similar to cilantro, though somewhat coarser and darker green. It doesn't bloom until its second year, however, and tends to be hardier and more tolerant of heat and drought. *Petroselinum crispum* var. *neopolitanum* is a flat-leafed variety with more concentrated flavor than curly-leafed parsley (the flat leaves are also less prone to sunburn and drought damage). The frilly cultivars are nevertheless garden-worthy for their beautiful foliage—just give them a little protection from full sun; 'Grüne Perle' is a low-growing German cultivar with deeply curled leaves that resemble a mound of moss. Good for much more than garnish, parsley adds its fresh flavor to fruit salads, soups, and pasta; it is also the "green" in the indispensible condiments Italian *salsa verde* and *gremolata*, French *sauce verte*, German *grüne sauce*, and others.

Rock Samphire | *Crithmum maritimum*

A rarity in North American gardens, rock samphire is an interesting, somewhat sprawling perennial (hardy in Zones 7 to 11) with umbels of white to greenish-yellow flowers and succulent gray-green leaves on stems 1 to 2 feet long. It hasn't hit the big time in American foodie circles but is well known in England and coastal Europe, where the strongly aromatic herb grows wild and is eaten raw in salads or pickled. It grows best in full sun and light soils with extremely good drainage. Its drought tolerance makes it good for rock gardens and seaside cottage gardens.

1 fennel, 2 lovage, 3 parsley, 4 flat-leaf parsley,
5 curly parsley, 6 rock samphire

Carrots | *Daucus carota* subsp. *sativus* var. *sativus*

The namesake plant of the carrot family, this easy-to-grow, sweet-tasting root vegetable is considered a "gateway" food for novice gardeners, veggie-phobic children, and health-minded sugar lovers alike. Once you start growing and eating carrots, other vegetables are likely to tempt you too. Like many other vegetables we grow for food today, carrots were first used as a medicinal plant and only later cultivated for substance and flavor.

It's true that the most colorful part of a carrot is out of sight until digging day, but the decorative value of the plant's ferny foliage shouldn't be underestimated. Canary-rooted 'Yellowstone' has a particularly lush, emerald top to 12 inches tall. 'Bolero', a famously tasty late-season carrot, also has thick top growth that discourages weeds. Plant them near nasturtiums for contrasting textures at the front of the border or in containers. Carrots are biennials; if not harvested, in their second growing season they will produce lacy umbels of delicate white flowers that draw pollinators and other beneficials to the garden.

Carrot seeds are tiny, so many suppliers offer them pelletized to make them easier to plant by hand. If your design calls for evenly spaced plants or geometric patterns, you can use seed tapes (bought or homemade). Plant seeds ¼ to ½ inch deep in early spring when the soil is 50°F or warmer, and then every month or so until late summer for successive harvests. They should germinate in one to three weeks and be ready to thin at about 2 inches tall to 2 inches apart. For straight, plump roots, grow them in deep, fertile, sandy, stone-free soil with regular moisture, and keep the early growth free of weeds—shredded straw makes a good mulch.

Nutritionally, carrots are among the few vegetables that are better for you cooked. More vitamin C is available in raw carrots, but heating frees up antioxidant

carotenoids for absorption by the body. Cooked or raw, carrots are also a good source of vitamin A, potassium, and fiber. In many cuisines, especially those of Europe, North Africa, and the Middle East, carrots provide a base note of earthy sweetness to savory stews and tagines, and they stand on their own roasted, steamed, and raw in salads.

Colorful carrots may or may not retain their hues after cooking. 'Purple Haze', a long dark purple carrot with a bright orange center, is stunning sliced up on a tray of crudités; its color fades when cooked beyond a light stir-fry. Slim, long, boldly sweet 'Red Samurai', retains its rosy-red color even after cooking. 'White Kuttinger' is an old Swiss cultivar that produces a white root.

Mediterranean herbs like sage (*Salvia officinalis*) and rosemary (*Rosmarinus officinalis*) welcome the radiant heat from walls and patios and will survive cold winters in pots indoors.

Herbs of the Mint Family

For thousands of years, people have cultivated aromatic plants of the mint family for culinary and medicinal reasons. Their obvious virtues in the kitchen and clinic notwithstanding, these plants can also be spectacular ornamentals, adding visual flair and texture to borders and containers. Despite similarities in flower shape and other characteristics that unite them in the Lamiaceae, mint family herbs are very diverse in appearance and habit, reflecting their wide adaptation worldwide—from temperate and tropical meadowlands to rocky, dry environments.

Growing Tips Many of the mint family herbs are warmth-loving Mediterranean perennials that are treated as annuals in North American edible landscapes. Most thrive in full sun and well-drained average soil with a pH around 6 to 7; use compost and top mulching to improve the tilth and keep down weeds. Once they are established, these herbs need little care; occasional shearing of woody stems encourages branching and leaf development. All these herbs benefit from frequent trimming to encourage growth of the aromatic foliage, which means at least modest harvests throughout the summer and fall. Fertilizing is usually not necessary and can actually dilute the aromatic volatile oils in the foliage. All mint family herbs need good ventilation to avoid mildew, and with the exception of some species of *Mentha*, moisture-retentive soils can lead to root rot.

Propagation Herbs in the mint family are easiest to propagate from stem cuttings or divisions; some, such as spearmint (*Mentha spicata*), are difficult to grow from seed and usually purchased as potted seedlings from nurseries. Peppermint, spearmint, and wild bergamot are rhizomatous and have a tendency to spread—the mints should be planted in containers to keep them in bounds. Divide plants every few years, either to rejuvenate or curb. Basil is the most tender of the mint family herbs and gardened as an annual. Plant seed or young starts after all chance of frost is past.

Harvesting and Eating Herbs are at their most fragrant just before blooming, so gardeners primarily interested in their culinary use will keep bloom spikes trimmed off. However, since most mint family herbs are perennials and continue to live on after flowering, it won't hurt to allow them to bloom—and further enhance the edible landscape. Mint family herbs are most flavorful used fresh, but they can also be dried or frozen for later use (freezing preserves the essential oils best). Use wild bergamot and spearmint leaves fresh or dried in tea and desserts, and add the fresh flowers to salads—these uses also apply to basil, with the addition of pesto. "Savory" herbs like oregano, rosemary, sage, thyme, and savory are strong, distinctive flavorings in beans, pasta sauces, and meats like beef, pork, and poultry.

Spearmint | *Mentha spicata*

Homemade mint tea, mojitos, and mint juleps are but three of the many reasons to grow your own spearmint. Given rich, moist soil and full to partial sun, spearmint has the ability to spread like wildfire where it's hardy (Zones 3 to 9). Keep it contained or you may soon find yourself in the mint-farming business. Spearmint cultivars include the handsome 'Kentucky Colonel', which grows 1 to 2 feet tall and wide, with 3-inch-long lance-shaped leaves and spikes of pale lilac flowers.

Peppermint | *Mentha × piperita*

Ubiquitous peppermint, flavoring everything from mouthwash to tooth-decaying confections, is a hybrid of spearmint (*Mentha spicata*) and water mint (*M. aquatica*). Like most mints, it must be kept in check to prevent its rampant spread. There are a number of interesting cultivars to try, for both decorative and culinary purposes: *M. × piperita* 'Chocolate Mint', 'Lime Mint', and 'Orange Mint' grow to about 2 feet tall with purple flowers, and all provide the promise of their names. 'Variegata' has attractive mottled yellow-and-green leaves. Peppermint is hardy in Zones 5 to 9.

Lemon Balm | *Melissa officinalis*

Tasty sprinkled fresh over fruit salad or dried for tea is ultrafragrant lemon balm. Bees are drawn to it too—as reflected in its genus name, *Melissa*, Greek for "honeybee."

Harvest the top growth of your lemon balm halfway through the summer to prevent it from flowering (they aren't ornamentally significant) and keep it bushy. It's hardy in Zones 3 to 7 as long as the soil doesn't become saturated.

Sweet Basil | *Ocimum basilicum*
Though it's native to India and Iran, you needn't live in a hot climate to have success growing basil as an annual: Rich soil, regular water, and a sunny location are all this herb desires. Sweet basil, a classic for pesto and other Italian fare, also has varieties and cultivars with subtle differences in flavor, such as licoricy 'Siam Queen', great for Thai and Vietnamese dishes. Among the most decorative cultivars are purple-leafed 'Red Rubin' and neat, small-leafed 'Pistou', which grows as a very dense, green globe—perfect for containers and formal situations.

Oregano | *Origanum vulgare*
Though generally low-sprawling and spreading, common oregano can grow to 18 inches tall, with lovely, long-blooming pinkish-mauve flowers. The dark green pungent leaves are used fresh or dried on pizza and in sauces, eggs, and meat dishes. Close relative Greek oregano (*Origanum vulgare* subsp. *hirtum*) is the real power hitter in the kitchen, though, with deeply aromatic leaves used in a multitude of cuisines, including Italian, Greek, and Middle Eastern. Hardy in Zones 4 to 8, both are fabulous for growing as groundcovers in well-drained soil.

Rosemary | *Rosmarinus officinalis*
An essential kitchen herb, rosemary is bliss on roasted vegetables, chicken, and lamb. In the garden, rosemary adds elegance and structure; its woody stems covered with grayish evergreen needlelike leaves may be grown as an upright rounded shrub, pruned as a topiary, or even allowed to trail along a wall or walk with a low-growing

1 spearmint, 2 peppermint, 3 lemon balm, 4 basil, 5 oregano, 6 rosemary

cultivar like 'Prostratus'. Gardeners in Zones 8 to 10 can plant rosemary in a sunny, well-drained spot and watch the plant grow to 6 feet tall over the years; colder-climate gardeners must pot it up before the first frost hits and overwinter it indoors or start again with a new plant in the spring.

Sage | *Salvia officinalis*

Sage is popular both as an ornamental and a flavoring for poultry, pork, breads, and beans. Compact and shrubby (to about 18 inches tall and wide), with gray-green, oblong leaves and spikes of lavender-blue flowers in late spring, it is a pleasing sight in the garden as well as dried in wreaths and floral arrangements. Among the prettiest culinary sages is 'Tricolor', which has striking gray-green leaves with white edges and purple stems that bleed pink and lavender into the foliage. It is hardy in Zones 6 to 9.

Thyme | *Thymus vulgaris*
Creeping Thyme | *Thymus serpyllum*

In addition to its ability to enhance eggs, seafood, roasted vegetables, and other savory foods, tiny-leafed gray-green to peridot-colored thyme is a mainstay of perennial gardens, adding color and texture and providing a refreshing contrast to larger-leafed and higher-reaching plants. Creeping thyme (*Thymus serpyllum*), has an even lower profile, making it a fine groundcover or rock garden plant. Most thymes are hardy in Zones 5 to 8 or 9.

Lavender | *Lavandula* species

Lavender flowers are not just suitable for fragrant sachets and dried arrangements: Fresh or dried, they can be an unexpected delight in sorbet, chocolate desserts, and savory foods like salads and stews. English lavender (*Lavandula angustifolia*) is the species most commonly used in cooking (it's a component of *herbs de Provence*): 'Rosea' is a pink-flowered cultivar; 'Munstead' has deep

1 sage, 2 thyme, 3 lavender, 4 wild bergamot, 5 summer savory, 6 giant blue hyssop

blue flowers on a compact plant. The hybrid *L. × intermedia* 'Hidcote Giant' grows to at least 40 inches tall and bears impressive spikes of lavender-purple blossoms. Lavender isn't very cold hardy, but most species can survive winters in Zones 7 to 9 and some to Zones 5 with protection.

Wild Bergamot, Bee Balm | *Monarda fistulosa*

This native wildflower has gray-green lance-shaped leaves and light purple flowers on long, upright stems to 4 feet tall. Its most common culinary use is as a honey plant, though Native American tribes enjoyed it in meat dishes and teas. It is hardy in Zones 3 to 9. A related species, *Monarda didyma*, produces red flowers and has a distinct citrus-mint flavor.

Winter Savory | *Satureja montana*

A short, bushy perennial (Zones 6 to 8) with small leaves and pale lilac flowers, winter savory works well at the front of the border. Its foliage has a spicy, peppery taste, welcome in poultry dishes or stuffings. Winter savory's relative *Satureja hortensis*, summer savory, is an annual with a more delicate flavor.

Giant Blue Hyssop | *Agastache foeniculum*

This North American native, with its late-summer spikes of purplish-blue flowers and medium-green leaves, can grow over 3 feet tall and works well in sunny borders in Zones 4 to 8. The licorice-mint-scented leaves and flowers can be steeped in water for tea or in milk for flavoring ice cream; they can also be chopped and sprinkled on savory meat and vegetable dishes.

Designing an Herb Garden

An herb is a plant that is useful as a seasoning, fragrance, dye, fiber, or medicine, and herb gardens have long combined practicality with beauty. In traditional dooryard gardens, plants that provide flavor are grown close to hand, and informal borders of sweet-smelling herbs frame intimate private pleasure gardens. In the Middle Ages, monks assembled medicinal plants in healing gardens near their infirmaries. During the Renaissance, herbs were grown and clipped into complex geometric patterns to make knot gardens, a convention that lives on today as one of the most ambitious herb garden designs.

Lately gardeners have become increasingly interested in the ornamental qualities of herbs. New color forms and cultivars of species long grown for their usefulness have been developed, while foliage plants that are considered herblike in texture, form, or fragrance as well as flowers and even vegetables are now admitted to the herb garden.

For inspiration and tips to plan your own herb garden and information on many more herb species and cultivars, see the Brooklyn Botanic Garden handbook *Designing an Herb Garden* (bbg.org/handbooks).

Lettuce

Lettuce (*Lactuca sativa*), first cultivated thousands of years ago in the Mediterranean and Near East, is a fast-growing and colorful annual with a variety of types—perfect for filling in holes early in the season while other plants are just getting going. Later, as the weather gets too warm for it to thrive in full sun, lettuce can grow tucked in under taller plants or in dappled shade. Frilly red-hued butterhead and multicolored cultivars of leaf lettuce are also great for defining borders in spring and again late in the season.

Growing Tips Most lettuces prefer cool weather and sandy or otherwise well-draining, slightly acidic soil, enriched with organic material. Since foliage growth is what you want, a high-nitrogen fertilizer such as fish emulsion or composted manure isn't out of order. Mulching will help keep the soil moist and deter soil-borne fungal diseases; watch out for slugs, aphids, and the occasional cutworm. For most lettuces, the summer's heat and longer days will prompt tall flower stalks to bolt up from the plant's center, contributing a week or so of yellow composite flowers to the garden as they signal an end to palatability. In warmer regions, look for heat-resistant, slow-bolting cultivars, especially of romaine, which handles heat better than most lettuces. In late August, more seeds can be sown for harvest well into fall; protection with cloches, row covers, or cold frames can extend the season even further.

Propagation Sow seed in the garden as soon as the soil can be worked (or in winter in Zones 8 to 10). Seeds can also be planted in flats several weeks before the last frost and hardened off before transplanting. Lettuce needs light to germinate, so barely cover seeds with a sprinkling of soil. Thin young plants when they're 2 to 4 inches high (for the first tender salad of the season); thin heading lettuces to about a foot apart. Plant seeds every two weeks until it stops coming up (lettuce won't germinate once the soil temperature rises above 75°F or so), then begin again late in the summer.

Harvesting and Eating Most lettuce varieties are very fast growing and can be harvested as microgreens within a few weeks of sprouting. Unless you're waiting for a full, tight head (50 to 75 days), lettuce is cut-and-come-again: Once the foliage is several inches tall, use a serrated knife to cut outer leaves and leave the inner rosette to continue growing. Even if you cut the entire plant down to about 2 inches above the ground, it will regrow if conditions are cool enough. Lettuce leaves become bitter as the weather heats up; once it bolts, pull it out and wait for the next crop. A large part of lettuce's culinary popularity is its mild flavor and ease of preparation. It is usually eaten raw with dressing, but it may also be served wilted with a hot vinaigrette or braised.

Colorful leaf lettuce, butterhead lettuce, lettuce allowed to bolt and set seed

Loose Leaf

Loose-leaf lettuce types are the easiest to grow, forming rosettes of loosely bunching foliage 6 to 10 inches tall and wide. Leaves are often ruffled or lobed like an oak leaf and may be anywhere from pale green to dark red. Among the more colorful loose-leaf lettuces are frilly-leafed bright red 'Vulcan', the dark maroon 'Red Velvet', and red lollo russo types (sometimes called lolla rossa), such 'Lollo Rosso Dark'.

Butterhead

Loose-heading butterhead (or Bibb) lettuce, with juicy, roundish leaves, grows best in cooler weather; it becomes bitter in warm conditions. Heirloom butterhead cultivars include the light yellow-green 'Gotte Jaune d'Or' and pink-tinged 'Brune d'Hiver'. 'Yugoslavian Red Butterhead' has red-tipped green outer leaves and a near-white core.

Romaine

Probably the most robustly flavored (and earliest cultivated) among the types of *Lactuca sativa*, romaine (or cos) grows upright 12-inch leaves in loose heads and is served both raw (in Caesar salad, for example) and braised. 'Rouge d'Hiver' is a red-leafed heirloom; 'Forellenschluss' is an Austrian heirloom with red-speckled light green leaves.

Crisphead

Sturdy iceberg (or crisphead) lettuces are latecomers, developed mainly for shipping long distances without drying out or browning; they generally grow 9 to 15 inches high and wide. 'Rouge Grenobloise' ('Red Grenoble') is a slow-bolting red-tinted iceberg; another slow bolter good for warm-climate gardens is green-leafed 'Webb's Wonderful'.

Pole Beans

Of the two main growth habits of common garden beans (*Phaseolus vulgaris*)—pole and bush—poles easily have it over bushes as edible landscape choices: They will bloom all summer if the pods are continuously harvested, producing a steady crop rather than one short flush, as bush types generally do; and they take up less room in the garden than bush beans. Clambering up tall tepees and trellises, their vining stems hidden amid lush, emerald three-part leaflets, exquisite little white or purple flowers, and long, dangling pods of green, yellow, maroon, or mottled purple—just begging to be picked—pole beans are emblematic of the ornamental edible garden.

Growing Tips Beans thrive in full sun and well-draining loamy soil enriched with compost, and a little lime if the pH falls below 6. Easy and fast growing, they are great starter annuals for neophyte gardeners. The hardest part is setting up the supports, which must be done before the seeds go in. Pole beans will grow 10 to 20 feet tall given the opportunity, but the supporting tripods, vertical poles, or trellises only need to be 6 to 8 feet tall; just make sure they are solid and stable enough to support a lot of biomass and won't blow over in the wind. The leafy vines will also create a fair amount of shade, so consider planting them near lettuce, chard, and other plants that appreciate less than a full day of open sun. A traditional combination, three sisters, calls for beans to be planted to twine up nearby cornstalks, their roots shaded by the large leaves of squash plants as they fix nitrogen in the soil.

Propagation Plant bean seeds 1 inch deep in spring, as soon as the soil is reliably over 65°F; they won't grow in cold soil. Water well and keep moist until they germinate, usually within a week or ten days.

Scarlet Runner Bean | *Phaseolus coccineus*

Named for its prominent bright red blossoms, which bloom all summer, scarlet runner is a spectacular ornamental edible. Planted in full sun in rich soil with regular moisture, it may grow to 20 feet tall and envelop an arched trellis or arbor in profuse foliage and flowers. It also makes a lovely privacy screen for a porch or boundary fence. The young pods can be eaten like green beans when very young (3 or 4 inches), before they grow fuzzy, tough, and a foot long (45 to 60 days). The large beans inside are tasty and pretty—black with magenta spots—and can be eaten fresh or dried.

Yellow, green, and purple pole beans

Harvesting and Eating Pick beans in the morning, before the heat of the day. Green beans, like most everything, taste best fresh, but they can also be canned or frozen after blanching. Harvest when about pencil-thick and lightly steam, stir-fry, or sauté with herbs. Or stew them with other ingredients like bacon and onions for a heartier dish. The classic storage food, shell beans can be eaten immediately or dried for rib-sticking winter dinners—chili, Boston baked beans, cassoulet, and nearly every culture's unique version of rice and beans.

Green, String, or Snap Bean

Beans have been cultivated in the Americas for many thousands of years and world-wide for centuries. As a result, hundreds of cultivars have been selected for storing dried as well as for eating fresh as pods—variously referred to as green, string, or snap beans; haricots verts; and flat wax beans. Pick them while they still "snap," before the pods become rubbery and tough. 'Kentucky Wonder', a favorite of generations of gardeners, produces tender, 9-inch green pods packed with extremely flavorful plump, brown beans (65 days).The heirloom 'Marvel of Venice' is a delicious flat yellow bean good for eating in the pod or shelled (60 to 70 days).

Shell Bean

Nearly all pole (and bush) beans can be eaten pod and all if picked early enough, when they are still tender. Left to grow on the vine, the pods will become tough and lumpy with the maturing beans inside. In late summer or early fall, the beans can be removed from the pods and either simmered for half an hour for dinner or blanched and frozen. For dried beans, leave the pods on the vine until they grow brown and the seeds rattle loose within. In humid or short-season climates, vines can be hung to dry in a cool, dry spot before being shelled. When the beans are rock hard, store them in an airtight jar and soak before cooking. 'Borlotto Solista' has beautiful white-mottled maroon pods; the kidney beans inside are opposite, white flecked with purple (85 days).

Strawberries

Easy to grow and beloved for their juicy, sweet fruit, strawberries are among the most popular perennials for kitchen gardens and patio containers, but their charming flowers, shiny three-part toothed leaves, and low-growing habit make them wonderful in ornamental situations too. Though less cultivated than the common garden strawberry, the smaller wild and woodland strawberries are prized for their tasty fruit and pretty flowers, which may be hues of pink as well as white. Plant them as edging for borders, along sidewalks, in baskets and containers, in rock gardens, and as a spreading, nearly evergreen groundcover in sunny and partly shady areas.

Growing Tips Strawberries grow best in rich, slightly acidic, sandy or well-drained soil in full sun. Mulch heavily, preferably with straw, to retain ground moisture and keep the fruit from touching the dirt and falling prey to slugs and snails. If birds discover the beds, spread bird netting over the plants during their peak production (more feasible for June-bearing types). Strawberries are prone to fungal diseases like *Verticillium* wilt, but many resistant cultivars are available.

Propagation Most strawberry cultivars are best purchased as young plants and set out in the garden in early spring or, in the South, fall. Dig a hole for each plant that is deep enough to accommodate the roots; mound soil in the center of the hole and drape the roots over the mound before filling, leaving the crown exposed at the surface. Wild and woodland strawberry seed is available for starting at home. Cold stratify the seeds for a couple of weeks before starting in flats indoors. Transplant outside in early spring when three sets of true leaves have developed. Most strawberries send out runners from which new plants develop; leave them to spread, or snip them off and replant where you want them. (Keeping runners clipped also redirects energy toward fruiting.)

Harvesting and Eating Some strawberry plants produce fruit heavily for a couple of weeks in late spring (standard, or June-bearing, varieties). Others bear lightly and steadily until frost sends them into dormancy (day neutral, or everbearing). Gently pluck each fruit by its stem just behind the calyx to avoid pulling off the entire cluster. Check the fruit clusters at least every other day (morning is best), and pick the strawberries as they are ready. For eating immediately—by themselves, over shortbread with a little crème fraîche, or whipped into a smoothie—pick the fruit when they are perfectly red and tender. If you want them for freezing or making jam, pick them when they are red but still rather firm. The leaves can also be used fresh or thoroughly dried to make tea.

Wild strawberry, garden strawberry

Garden Strawberry | *Fragaria × ananassa*

Most of the strawberries we grow and eat today are cultivars of *Fragaria × ananassa*, an 18th-century cross of two New World species, *F. chiloensis* (beach strawberry) and *F. virginiana* (wild strawberry). These plants grow 6 to 12 inches high and wide and tend not to send out as many runners as straight species. 'Ozark Beauty' (Zones 4 to 8) is a disease-resistant day-neutral cultivar that produces a good crop in June and another in early fall, with light fruiting in between. If ornamental value takes precedence, *F. × ananassa* 'Frel' (PINK PANDA) has medium-pink flowers and occasional small fruit; 'Variegata' has green and white leaves and white flowers. For large berries on a disease- and heat-resistant day-neutral plant, try *F. × ananassa* 'Seascape'.

Wild Strawberry | *Fragaria virginiana*

A North American native, wild strawberry grows low and spreads far, with runners up to 2 feet long that carry with them baby plants (for this reason it's considered a weed in the Northeast). Wild strawberry fruits are much smaller than those of its offspring *F. × ananassa* but have a concentrated sweetness that appeals to a host of wildlife as well as humans. 'Little Scarlet' is a short-season producer used to make the delicious and hard-to-find Tiptree "Little Scarlet" Strawberry Preserves (a favorite of none other than James Bond).

Woodland, Alpine Strawberry | *Fragaria vesca*

Most woodland strawberries have an upright habit with few or no runners. There are both spring-bearing and day-neutral forms. *Fragaria vesca* f. *semperflorens* 'Yellow Wonder' is day neutral and has small, cream-colored sweet-tasting fruit that are reportedly ignored by birds; *F. vesca* 'Lipstick' has rose-red blossoms that bloom (and fruit) all season; 'Rügen', another day-neutral woodland, has an upright habit, grows about 8 inches high, and spreads well to fill in rock gardens and borders.

Table Grapes

Picture the ultimate lifestyle magazine spread: a long rustic dining table at which are gathered an extended family enjoying a home-grown feast—the entire tableau shaded from the late-afternoon sun by a sturdy old arbor of lush grapevines, its clusters of dusky green and purple fruits dangling romantically. The scene could be in Nyack as easily as Naples: Table grapes, the best ones for eating rather than winemaking, are happy to grow almost everywhere. Native to North America as well as Eurasia and the Middle East, grapes for thousands of years have symbolized hospitality and bounty—what better reason to invite them into your garden?

Growing Tips Grapevines, woody perennials hardy at least in Zones 5 to 8, aren't very particular about soil, as long as it is deep and well draining, but they do need full sun to reliably produce tasty fruit. Plant vines in fall or early spring, making sure the graft union is above the soil. Set each plant with plenty of room to spread out—vines can grow 10 to 20 feet wide and 10 feet tall or more. Provide sturdy supports at planting time to avoid disturbing the roots as the vine burgeons. Prune back to one stem and two buds; as the vine matures, let it develop a few lateral branches, and prune it severely during winter dormancy to train it and improve productivity. Fruit develops on year-old wood; once the vine is shaped, retain well-spaced "renewal buds" to form fruit.

Propagation Grape plants are usually available from nurseries as one- or two-year grafted plants. Ask your local Cooperative Extension to suggest cultivars that are resistant to insects and fungal diseases in your area before ordering catalog plants. Most varieties, except some muscadines (*Vitis rotundifolia*), are self-pollinating.

Hardy Kiwi | *Actinidia arguta*, *A. deliciosa*

A relative novelty in American gardens, the woody, deciduous kiwi vine, a native of northeastern Asia, is becoming popular for arbors and screens in Zones 4 to 8. Small, fragrant white flowers appear among 3- to 5-inch dark green leaves in early summer, and fruits ripen in fall (150 days). Unlike the brown, fuzzy, egg-size fruit of *Actinidia chinensis*,

 those of hardy kiwi are smooth, green, and don't need peeling. Kiwis are generally sold as two-year-old grafted bare-root plants and should be planted in deep, rich, moist but well-drained soils on the acid side in full sun. They are dioecious and require both male and female plants blooming simultaneously to achieve fruit set. Over time, they may reach 30 feet or more. Like grapes, kiwi vines produce fruit on second-year wood and need conscientious pruning.

Muscadine grape, wine grape

Harvesting and Eating Most table grapes ripen in late summer into fall. The best way to determine a grape's ripeness is to taste it for the right balance of sweet and tart. The seeds, if there are any, should be dark. Never pull grapes from the vine; use scissors or pruners to clip the clusters near the branch. Old World grapes (*Vitis vinifera*) can be refrigerated for a few weeks, but fox grapes *(V. labrusca)* and other "slip-skin" North American grapes should be eaten right away or made into jelly, jam, juice, or dried for raisins. If you have the inclination and a huge amount of grapes, you can even make wine with them. Grape leaves are delicious brined and stuffed with seasoned rice.

New World Grapes | *Vitis labrusca, V. rotundifolia*
Cultivars derived from North American species have natural resistance to certain pests like phylloxera and generally grow well as long as conditions aren't too humid. *Vitis labrusca*, fox grape, so called for its musky scent, is native from the eastern seaboard (except Florida) to the Mississippi. Cold hardy and disease resistant, it is the parent of 'Concord', famous for flavoring jelly. Muscadine (*V. rotundifolia*) grows wild in the Southeast as far west as Texas and Missouri (Zones 6 to 9); it's not as cold hardy but just as disease and pest resistant as the fox grape. 'Carlos' is a bronze-colored scuppernong type; 'Nesbitt' is a tasty black grape—both can produce fruit with only one vine.

Old World Grapes | *Vitis vinifera*
Many Old World, or wine, grapes are also good for eating fresh and have been hybridized with American species for better hardiness and disease resistance; almost all vines are also now grown on rootstock of New World grapes for this reason. Seedless selections include the popular raisin grape 'Thompson Seedless'; 'Lakemont', which has yellow-green late-summer fruit; and 'Suffolk Red' (sometimes listed as 'Suffolk'), which has tender-skinned red fruit.

Tomatoes

Native to the tropical highlands of South America, where it has been eaten for thousands of years, the tomato (*Solanum lycopersicum*) was slowly popularized in other parts of the world starting 500 years ago. In the past century the tomato has become the most consumed "vegetable" (botanically it's a berry) in the United States, valued for its vitamin C and lycopine content as well as its flavor. Whether your garden calls for neatly pruned plants trellised against a sunny wall or clusters of fruit cascading riotously from a hanging basket, there are hundreds of heirlooms and hybrids to suit your situation—and your tastebuds.

Growing Tips Tomatoes prefer full sun, ideally in rich, loamy to sandy soil with a pH of 6 to 7. Transplant seedlings only after all chance of frost is past; tomatoes are very tender and need warm soil and air. Add a handful of well-rotted manure to the planting hole, and top-dress in midseason with compost tea or fish emulsion. Cool nights can cause poor fruit set; try draping the plants at night with a sheet or wrapping the tomato cages with clear plastic until the weather becomes reliably warm.

Tomatoes are either determinate or indeterminate. Determinate types generally have a compact, bushy habit—after blooming they stop growing and decline once the fruit is ripe, usually over a few weeks in early to midseason. Indeterminate tomatoes (including almost all heirlooms) grow and fruit continuously and have a rampant vining habit that requires support unless you prefer to let them sprawl; they can be staked, caged, or trellised at the time of transplanting and pruned to one or two stems (or not).

Propagation Start seeds indoors, on a heating pad if possible, with lots of light, four to six weeks before last frost. After the last frost date, harden off before transplanting into the garden. If buying plant starts at your local nursery, don't be tempted by the ones with blooms—tomato plants are stressed by transplanting, and those flowers and fruits are likely to drop. Look for leafy dark green plants 6 to 8 inches tall. Seeds of heirlooms can be dried for future use; they will usually come true to seed; seeds of hybrids will not.

Harvesting and Eating Regardless of its color, a tomato may be deemed ripe when it's slightly soft to the touch and has a sweet aroma. It should practically drop off the vine when you touch it, but if not, gently twist or cut the stem without pulling. Those you don't slice and serve still warm from the sun with olive oil and salt (and perhaps a dribble of balsamic vinegar) can be frozen whole, blanched and peeled for canning or sauce making, or cut into pieces for dehydrating. Tomatoes are best ripened on the vine, but if necessary they can be picked a little early and ripened on a windowsill. Green tomatoes are also delicious sliced and fried in cornmeal batter or made into chutney or pickles.

Globe, cherry, and plum tomatoes

Cherry

These bite-size fruits (sometimes listed as *Solanum lycopersicum* var. *cerasiforme*) make healthy snacks, set off green salads, and fit beautifully on skewers for grilling. 'Chadwick' grows to a vigorous 5 feet tall with prolific fruit to 1½ inches across (indeterminate); 'Chocolate Cherry', 3 to 6 feet tall, produces 1-inch fruits that are a rich brownish-plum color inside and out (indeterminate). Dwarf cultivars good for windowsills and containers include 'Tiny Tim', which grows only about 1½ feet tall, with cherry-size red fruit (determinate), and 'Gold Nugget', 2 to 3 feet tall, with dark yellow tomatoes (determinate).

Plum

Also called paste tomatoes, plums have denser flesh and less juice than other varieties, which makes them good for canning whole and cooking into sauce. 'Roma' is one of the most popular cultivars, with firm, egg-shaped light to dark red fruits on 3- to 4-foot vines (indeterminate); more ornamental cultivars include 'Striped Roman', red with orange striations (indeterminate), and 'Banana Legs', which has long, 4-inch golden fruit, great for processing or eating out of hand (determinate).

Globe

Growing on vines 3 to 5 feet tall, these medium-size, usually smooth, round tomatoes can ripen as early as midsummer and are the most commonly grown type of tomato. Juicy yet sliceable, they are very versatile in the kitchen and have been widely cultivated for flavor and showiness. The 8- to 10-ounce 'Spears Tennessee Green' ripens to emerald green at the top, fading to amber toward the bottom (indeterminate).

Beefsteak

Many beefsteak cultivars are heirlooms almost as beloved for their lumpy misshapen bulk as for their rich tomato flavor. The fruit of 'Brandywine', perhaps the most popular heirloom tomato in cultivation, has deep pink skin and red flesh and may weigh a pound at maturity; its meaty flesh is a balance of sweet and acid (indeterminate).

Spicy-tasting, colorful flowers like 'Tangerine Gem' signet marigold (*Tagetes tenuifolia*) add vibrancy to the verdure of an ornamental potager.

Edible Flowers

Tucked along borders and in among the lush and nourishing greens, fruits, herbs, and root vegetables of the edible landscape are vivid edible flowers like pansies, nasturtiums, and marigolds. Amid the flowers of umbels, mints, and bolting brassicas, these heavy bloomers add visual and culinary zest to salads, desserts, pickles, and jams.

There are a few important rules for eating flowers: First, don't pick anything you aren't sure is edible. Just because you saw it garnishing a dish somewhere doesn't mean it's okay to eat. There are many good reference books and websites that provide lists of both poisonous and edible flowers. Second, be sure of your source. Only eat flowers that have been organically grown; nursery or florist plants are often treated with external or systemic herbicides and fertilizers unsafe for human consumption. Don't eat flowers from roadsides or waste ground—besides surface pollution like car exhaust and pet waste, goodness knows what toxins are in the soil.

Growing Tips The plants described in this sampling are either true annuals or tender perennials treated as annuals in North American gardens. Most thrive in full sun, in rich, moist but well-draining, slightly acidic soils—the same conditions your vegetable and fruit plants prefer. Mulch to keep down weeds, retain moisture, and keep mud and sand from splashing up on the flowers. As blooming commences, deadhead spent blossoms to keep the plants flowering all summer. While you're at it, keep an eye out for pests such as snails and slugs, which can be picked off by hand, and aphids, which a light blast with the hose will dislodge (take care with buds).

Propagation Many edible flowers are popular bedding plants and are widely available for spring planting. However, unless you can be sure they have been organically grown, it's advisable to propagate the plants from seed or home cuttings if you intend to eat their flowers. Whether the seeds need to be started indoors or planted directly in the garden depends on their hardiness and days to bloom, so plan ahead.

Harvesting and Eating Cut flowers early in the morning after the dew has evaporated, gently shaking off any insects. Keep stemmed flowers in a vase of water in a cool place. Flowers plucked without the stem, such as borage and nasturtium, should be picked as close to the time of use as possible; otherwise store them in a plastic bag on a damp paper towel in the fridge for up to a week. Except for violas, borage, impatiens, and nasturtiums, which taste and look fine whole, separate flower petals from the sepals and remove their bitter white bottom edges before using them as garnish or strewing them over food. Removing the pistils and stamens from these flowers also helps avoid allergic reactions from pollen.

Borage | *Borago officinalis*
Rangy, fuzzy borage has one of the rare true blue flowers, and though considered a vegetable in its native Syria and in Europe, it's used more as a decorative floral garnish in American kitchens, sprinkled on salads and candied for dessert decoration. Plant seeds about ⅛-inch deep as soon as all danger of frost has passed where you want it to grow—it doesn't like transplanting. Borage easily grows 2 feet tall and may need support. It readily self-seeds and will pop up nearby in following years.

Calendula, Pot-Marigold | *Calendula officinalis*
The large, bright yellow to orange, single or double composite flowers of this old-fashioned garden flower arrive early in the summer and are among the last flowers blooming in fall. Plant seeds ¼ inch deep in early spring (or fall in Zones 8 to 10) in a fertile, sunny bed or container. Most cultivars grow to about a foot tall, with long green leaves. The lightly spicy-bitter petals may be used as a substitute for saffron to color egg and rice dishes and accent salads and soups. Calendula is also used as a medication for skin ailments.

Clove Pink, Hardy Carnation | *Dianthus caryophyllus*
This cutting (and eating) flower has blue-green foliage and stems from 6 to 24 inches tall or more, depending on the cultivar, upon which bloom frilly- or simple-petaled round flowers that may be single or double and shades of white, pink, or red with

darker-hued centers. Native to the Mediterranean, it is hardy in Zones 7 to 10 and often grown as an annual. Sow seeds indoors and plant seedlings after all danger of frost is past in sunny, neutral, freely draining soil. The flower adds a sweet clove flavor to confections and beverages, though scent and taste may have been bred out of some cultivars grown for color or other traits. 'Enfant de Nice' (mixed colors) and 'Fenbow Nutmeg Clove' (dark red flowers) are highly scented cultivars.

Scented Geranium | *Pelargonium* species and hybrids

Ranging from subtle, delicate evocations of rose, apple, and chocolate to pungent citrus, ginger, pineapple, and combinations thereof, you have your choice of essences among scented geraniums. Tender South African perennials treated as annuals above Zone 8 (or brought indoors during winter), scented geraniums thrive in well-drained average soil in bright light with some protection from the hottest afternoon sun. Geraniums can be grown from seed but are best rooted from cuttings. Use the blossoms in salads and as garnishes, and steep them with the leaves to flavor ice creams, sugars, and savory dishes.

Impatiens | *Impatiens walleriana*

The most popular bedding plant in America, low, spreading impatiens bloom all summer in shady areas where other flowers and vegetables won't perform. Sow seeds indoors 6 to 8 weeks before last frost, just pressing them onto the soil (they need light to germinate), and transplant in late spring. Pinch plants back for bushy growth and watch out for slugs and snails. The flowers don't have much scent or flavor, but their myriad colors make them attractive scattered in salads and candied on confections.

Signet Marigold | *Tagetes tenuifolia*

This easy-to-grow Central American plant has ferny foliage on plants 6 to 8 inches tall and single or double flowers that usually bloom in a range from light yellow

1 borage, 2 calendula, 3 clove pink, 4 scented geranium, 5 scented geranium, 6 impatiens

to dark orange. Plant seeds directly in containers or at the front of beds around the last frost date. Fast growing and disease free, they will continue blooming into fall as long as faded flowers are deadheaded. The petals have a mildly bitter, citrusy flavor.

Nasturtium | *Tropaeolum majus*

With white-veined green peltate leaves and red, yellow, and orange frilly petaled, spurred flowers to 3 inches across from midsummer to fall, nasturtiums are an old-fashioned favorite for containers, hanging baskets, and cottage garden borders. Bushing types may grow to 1½ feet tall and wide; climbers will trail to 8 feet. Plant the seed of this easy-to-grow South American annual in the garden around the last frost. Nasturtiums like sunny, not-too-hot weather but can withstand partial shade, dry conditions, and lean soil (too much nitrogen produces lots of foliage and few flowers). 'Jewel Mix' is compact with double flowers; 'Alaska' has variegated leaves. The peppery-tasting flowers and leaves add punch to salads, and the pickled seedpods resemble capers in taste.

Pansy, Johnny Jump-up, Sweet Violet
Viola species and hybrids

Whether planted in rows as border edgings, flowing from containers, or free-seeded throughout the garden, garden pansies (*Viola* × *wittrockiana*), Johnny jump-ups (*V. tricolor*), and sweet violets (*V. odorata*) are indispensable in the edible landscape. Plant seeds in the garden in fall and let them overwinter beneath heavy mulch or under a cold frame. Garden pansies and Johnny jump-ups are low-growing short-lived perennials usually treated as annuals; deadhead pansies to keep them blooming over three seasons. Violets are spring-blooming perennials in Zones 5 to 10. Crystallize them in sugar for decorating cakes or add them raw to fruit and green salads. Sweet violets are especially flavorful and are made into vinegars, dressings, and syrup for drinks, sorbets, and candy.

1 signet marigold, 2 nasturtium, 3, Johnny jump-up,
4 sweet violet, 5 sunflower, 6 sweet woodruff

Sunflower | *Helianthus annuus*

Sunflowers have been beloved in North American gardens since pre-Columbian times. They are easy to grow and start blooming within 60 to 100 days, their yellow-, orange-, or maroon-petaled flower heads (composed of many tiny disk and ray flowers) on high-reaching stems creating cheerful focal points in the garden. Provided with rich, well-drained soil and full sun, some cultivars can reach over 12 feet tall. The highly nutritious hard-shelled seeds can be harvested in late summer after the petals fade and the heavy seed heads droop; protect the drying kernels from birds with netting. Sunflowers that produce gray-striped seeds are usually the biggest and easiest to crack open. 'Mongolian Giant' grows to 14 feet tall and has flower heads 18 inches in diameter and 1½-inch gray-striped seeds.

Sweet Woodruff | *Galium odoratum*

Grown since ancient times for its sweet, hay-smelling whorled foliage and lovely starlike white flowers in April and May, sweet woodruff is a beautiful perennial groundcover 4 to 10 inches tall that thrives in moist, partially sunny to shady spots (Zones 4 to 8). Once established, it can become invasive if it likes its conditions, but trimming with a mower helps control it. Sow seed in the garden in early spring and keep it moist until established. The flowers and leaves are used to flavor white wine and other beverages and desserts.

Other Edible Blossoms

The flowers of many food plants are edible, including those of alliums; mint family herbs like sage, rosemary, and basil; and most carrot family herbs. Even the huge yellow blossoms of squash can be stuffed and fried like fritters. (An important

exception is the nightshade and potato family, including tomatoes, eggplants, peppers, and potatoes, most of whose flowers are toxic.) Herbal flowers tend to share the flavor of the leaves to a lesser or greater extent—taste before you throw them into salads, vinegars, and pickle mixes. Other flowers like roses and orange blossoms impart their unique floral perfume to food, adding their subtle, complex essence to desserts, salads, and beverages.

Salad with borage, calendula petals, and pansies

And Don't Miss...

Here are some of the other striking edible plants featured in this book's garden designs.

Asparagus | *Asparagus officinalis*

Ferny, tall, and long lived (10 to 30 years), this herbacious perennial is planted for the ages, so plan its site carefully. Asparagus is very hardy (Zones 2 to 9) but needs deep, very fertile, well-draining near-neutral soil in full sun. Purchasing year-old root crowns is easier for most home gardeners than starting asparagus from seed. (Most asparagus plants sold today are hybrid males, which have a longer life span than females but lack their decorative red fall berries.) Plant in early spring; spindly stems emerge the first season and grow thicker and taller in successive years, to 6 feet tall or more. Light harvesting is possible the second spring after planting, and yield increases over time.

Corn, Maize | *Zea mays*

Rising tall on its slender stalk, its long leaves arching gracefully, corn adds an undeniably elegant textural accent at the back of the border or in the center of a large container. Its very silhouette is emblematic of sustenance—it has been a staple food crop in the Americas for millennia and worldwide for 500 years. Corn needs nitrogen-rich soil, plenty of sun, and regular moisture to produce plump, full-kerneled ears. Plant seed 1 to 2 inches deep in spring when the soil is reliably 60°F or warmer, and later thin to 8 to 10 inches apart. Plants may grow anywhere from 2 to 12 feet tall, be single-stalked or multibranched, and produce edible corn in 60 to 120 days. When kernels are just tender and milky, they're ready. 'Chires Baby' (75 to 85 days) is a multi-branched variety that grows 4 to 5 feet tall and produces as many as 30 tiny ears, which when picked very young may be eaten cob and all.

1 asparagus, 2 corn, 3 fern fiddleheads, 4 fern fronds, 5 fig, 6 Jerusalem artichoke flower

Fiddlehead | *Matteuccia struthiopteris*

Tightly coiled fiddleheads, the emergent fronds of this beautiful vase-shaped fern, are favorite quarry of early-spring woodland foragers, before the fronds unfurl and develop into the inedible tall plumes that give it its other common name, ostrich fern. It is hardy in Zones 3 to 7 and thrives in full to partial shade in moist to wet soils, spreading slowly into a patch over time. Ferns are usually purchased as container plants and transplanted in the early spring. The next spring after they are established, the young fiddleheads may be lightly harvested; cut at ground level no more than three of the seven emergent fronds if you want the plant to survive. After removing any yellow or brown parts and washing thoroughly, boil or steam the fiddleheads and serve with a vinaigrette or cheese sauce.

Fig | *Ficus carica*

Among the oldest fruit trees in cultivation, figs make beautiful garden plants, their deeply lobed large leaves forming tiers along multiple branches, with brown, pink, bronze, or dark purple fruits ripening in the leaf axils in summer into fall. Figs have been bred to grow well beyond their native Mediterranean range; though generally hardy in Zones 8 to 10, some cultivars, such as copper-fruited 'Brown Turkey', will survive Zone 5 winters with adequate protection or against a heat-collecting wall. Figs may grow 10 to 30 feet tall and wide, but for tight spaces they can be kept pruned or root-bound in containers. The fruits are ready to pick when plump and soft to the touch, with syrup crystals beading on the skin; eat out of hand or make into jam and confections. Figs are relatively pest and disease free, but netting may be necessary to deter birds.

Jerusalem Artichoke | *Helianthus tuberosus*

Neither a true artichoke nor from Israel, the North American native Jerusalem artichoke is cultivated for its knobby edible tubers, also called sunchokes. Resembling

1 Malabar spinach, 2 okra flower, 3 okra, 4 pawpaw, 5 passion vine flower, 6 pea flower

its cousin the sunflower (*Helianthus annuus*), Jerusalem artichoke grows on a densely leafed sturdy stalk 3 to 10 feet tall, which is topped in midsummer with branching stems of yellow flowers 2 to 4 inches in diameter. In early spring, plant the tubers 4 inches deep, 1 to 2 feet apart, in a sunny spot in rich, well-draining soil where they won't shade out other sun-loving plants. Harvest the tubers in late fall; any little fragment left unearthed will winter over to grow a new plant where hardy (Zones 3 to 9). It readily spreads and is considered a weed in some states. 'Red Fuseau' produces small, round reddish-purple tubers that are not as knobby as other varieties, and thus easier to peel and prepare for cooking.

Malabar Spinach | *Basella alba*
The nutritious, semisucculent dark green leaves of sun-loving Malabar spinach fill the gap between spring and late-summer plantings of salad greens. This vining tropical native of India and Southeast Asia has a bushy, twining habit that makes it great for space-tight vertical gardens. Grow this tender perennial as an annual in full sun and rich soil, preferably with support such as a trellis or tomato cage to keep it from sprawling. The mild, earthy-flavored leaves and stems can begin to be harvested about two months after planting; they will continue to grow until frost. 'Rubra' has red-tinged leaves and stems.

Okra | *Abelmoschus esculentus*
Okra has been grown in North America since the late 1600s, most likely introduced from Africa with the slave trade. Sturdy stemmed, upright, and growing 2 to 5 feet tall, okra plants have attractive maplelike leaves and large ivory, yellow, or pinkish trumpet-shaped flowers that last only a day or so before wilting. The green or purple fingerlike pods that develop are picked young and tender for frying or grilling and to flavor and thicken gumbo and other stews. Pods left on the plant to dry provide visual interest long after the growing season ends and can be used in dried flower arrangements. Plant out seedlings only after days—and nights—are warm. It prefers full sun and light, well-draining, fertile soil. The highly ornamental dwarf cultivar 'Little Lucy' (50 days) has purple-tinged foliage and prolific yellow flowers with purple centers that produce 4-inch-long maroon pods.

Passion Flower, Maypop | *Passiflora incarnata*
Native to the southeastern United States, this beautiful, fast-growing tendriling vine makes a wonderful porch screen where its three-lobed dark green leaves and exquisite fringed white and lavender to dark purple, fragrant flowers can be admired up close. It may be grown as a perennial in Zones 5 to 9 from stratified seed but is more often grown by home gardeners from nursery plants. In winter, the vine may die back to the roots, but it returns in the spring, sometimes so vigorously that it can be invasive. Round to egg-shaped green "maypop" fruits ripen to yellow by early fall and can be eaten fresh or made into jelly.

Pawpaw | *Asimina triloba*

The multistemmed, suckering habit of this eastern North American native makes it a good candidate for an understory shrub or small tree in larger gardens in Zones 5 to 9, where it may grow to 20 feet tall and wide or more. Interesting cup-shaped maroon flowers dangle from the bare branches in midspring and develop into large, oblong chartreuse fruits that ripen to a speckled dark yellow or yellow-green in the autumn before the tropically large, deciduous leaves turn coppery gold. Pawpaw generally requires both a male and female plant for fruit set. It prefers well-draining, deep, near-neutral soil in sun or partial shade; from seed, it may take six to eight years to fruit.

Pea | *Pisum sativum*

The season for green, or English, peas is very short and very early, but the tender, sweet pods and immature seeds are worth gardening in chilly weather; plant the seeds in well-draining loam as soon as the soil can be worked. Peas may be low-growing plants or tendriling climbers that need to be supported by a fence or trellis. *Pisum sativum* var. *macrocarpon* 'Sugar Snap' is an award-winning cultivar that grows to 6 feet if the weather stays cool and its tender roots and stems are protected. When the pods start coming in thick and fast, harvest every day; those you don't eat right away can be blanched and frozen to retain their sweetness.

Persimmon | *Diospyros virginiana*

Its upright habit (to 60 feet tall and 35 feet wide in the wild) and tolerance of heat and drought make the American persimmon tree a good choice for urban gardens if its tendency for suckering is curbed. Like the pawpaw, the persimmon is native to the eastern half of the country (and can be grown in Zones 5 to 9); it is also usually dioecious and needs both male and female trees to fruit. For reliably tasty fruit, purchase grafted cultivars and plant in sandy soil and full sun to partial shade with lots of moisture until established; the tree should start producing within four to six years. Small green globelike fruits about 2 inches across form after the fragrant, greenish-white flowers fade in late spring and are notoriously astringent before they ripen in late fall to a dark burnt-orange or purple color.

Rhubarb | *Rheum rhabarbarum*

Like asparagus, rhubarb is a long-lived hardy perennial (Zones 3 to 9) and needs a large, permanent bed of deep, loamy, weed-free soil prepared for it. Plant rhizomes or divisions about 3 feet apart in spring as soon as the ground can be worked. Female plants of heirloom cultivars produce tall flower stalks, which should be cut off to extend foliage vigor. In following years, round red nodes appear at soil level, heralding the coming of tart, juicy red leaf stems (petioles). Harvest the stems lightly the first year and more heavily in successive years until they become thin in summer. Cut the stem near ground level or grab the stem at its base and gently tug it straight up. Remove the poisonous green, leafy part before using the stems in cobblers, preserves, and sauces.

Sorrel | *Rumex acetosa, R. sanguineus, R. scutatus*

Garden sorrel (*Rumex acetosa*) and French sorrel have been used as a nutritious potherb and salad green for millennia in their native Europe and eastern Asia. Because it wilts quickly, sorrel is not often found in American markets, all the more reason to grow it yourself. Sorrel is reliably perennial in Zones 5 to 8 and can be divided every few years. Harvest outside leaves from late spring on to keep the foliage dense and tender. *Rumex scutatus* 'Silver Buckler' has roundly shield-shaped leaves flecked with silver; *R. sanguineus* (blood sorrel) has long, bright green leaves with maroon stems and red veining. Its mature foliage is usually too tough and bitter to eat, but the tangy young leaves can be used as a microgreen.

Tomatillo | *Physalis philadelphica*

Tomatillos have a tangy green-tomato flavor and are used in Latin American and Southwestern dishes like *salsa verde*. Start seeds indoors as you would tomatoes, with a few extra days of hardening off before transplanting (these hot weather lovers require temperatures above 70°F). The 2- to 4-foot plant's branches can be brittle, so caging is a good idea. The yellowish-green fruit, which are about the size of golf balls, are covered with a papery green husk that turns brown and splits open with maturity; using garden scissors, harvest tomatillos as they ripen to encourage more fruiting.

Wintergreen | *Gaultheria procumbens*

Wintergreen is a fantastic four-season shrubby groundcover for gardens in Zones 3 to 8, growing 6 inches tall with glossy red-tinged evergreen leaves that give off a minty scent. Tiny white urn-shaped summer flowers are followed by bright red fruit that persist through winter. Wintergreen will grow in full sun but prefers moist, shade-dappled woodland conditions. Its dried leaves can be used to make a bracing flavoring for tea, hence one of its (many) common names, eastern teaberry.

1 persimmon, 2 rhubarb flowers, 3 rhubarb leaves,
4 blood sorrel, 5 tomatillo, 6 wintergreen

Edible Garden Plants at a Glance

The plants incorporated in this book's garden designs and profiled in the encyclopedia are listed below. We've indicated those species that are native to North America, grow well in sites with less than six hours of sun, and are great options for gardening with children.

N = North American Native   ☺ = Great for Kids   ◗ = Okay for Shade or Part Shade

ANNUALS (includes biennials and tender perennials grown as annuals in USDA Zones 4 through 6)

Abelmoschus esculentus	okra	Malvaceae		
Allium ampeloprasum var. *porrum*	leek	Alliaceae		
Allium ampeloprasum var. *ampeloprasum*	elephant garlic, broadleaf wild leek	Alliaceae		
Allium cepa	onion	Alliaceae		
Allium cepa var. *aggregatum*	shallot	Alliaceae		
Allium fistulosum	scallion, green onion, bunching onion, Welsh onion	Alliaceae		☺
Allium sativum	garlic	Alliaceae		
Amaranthus tricolor	Joseph's coat	Amaranthaceae		☺
Ananas comosus	pineapple	Bromeliaceae		
Anethum graveolens	dill	Apiaceae		☺
Anthriscus cerefolium	chervil	Apiaceae		
Basella alba	Malabar spinach	Basellaceae		◗
Beta vulgaris	beet	Chenopodiaceae		☺
Beta vulgaris var. *cicla*	chard	Chenopodiaceae		☺
Borago officinalis	borage	Boraginaceae		◗
Brassica juncea	mustard greens	Brassicaceae		
Brassica oleracea var. *acephala*	collards	Brassicaceae		
Brassica oleracea var. *botrytis*	cauliflower, romanesco	Brassicaceae		
Brassica oleracea var. *capitata*	cabbage	Brassicaceae		
Brassica oleracea (Gemmifera group)	brussels sprouts	Brassicaceae		
Brassica oleracea var. *gongylodes*	kohlrabi	Brassicaceae		
Brassica oleracea var. *italica*	broccoli	Brassicaceae		☺
Brassica oleracea var. *sabellica*	kale	Brassicaceae		☺
Calendula officinalis	pot-marigold	Asteraceae		
Capsicum annuum	ancho, jalapeño, serrano pepper	Solanaceae		
Capsicum chinense	Scotch bonnet, habanero pepper	Solanaceae		
Celosia argentea	plumed cockscomb	Amaranthaceae		☺
Citrullus lanatus	watermelon	Cucurbitaceae		☺
Coriandrum sativum	cilantro, coriander	Apiaceae		
Crithmum maritimum	rock samphire	Apiaceae		
Cucumis melo	melon	Cucurbitaceae		
Cucumis sativus	cucumber	Cucurbitaceae		☺
Cucurbita pepo	summer squashes, winter squashes, zucchini	Cucurbitaceae	N	☺
Cucurbita maxima	winter squashes	Cucurbitaceae		

Scientific name	Common name	Family			
Cucurbita moschata	winter squashes	Cucurbitaceae	N		
Cuminum cyminum	cumin	Apiaceae			
Daucus carota subsp. *sativus* var. *sativus*	carrot	Apiaceae		☺	
Dianthus caryophyllus	clove pink, carnation	Caryophyllaceae			
Elettaria cardamomum	cardamom	Zingiberaceae			◐
Helianthus annuus	sunflower	Asteraceae		☺	
Impatiens walleriana	impatiens	Balsaminaceae			◐
Ipomoea batatas	sweet potato	Convolvulaceae			
Lactuca sativa	lettuce	Asteraceae		☺	◐
Levisticum officinale	lovage	Apiaceae			
Momordica charantia	bitter melon	Cucurbitaceae			
Ocimum basilicum	sweet basil	Lamiaceae		☺	
Pelargonium species	scented geranium	Geraniaceae		☺	◐
Petroselinum crispum	parsley	Apiaceae			◐
Phaseolus coccineus	scarlet runner bean	Fabaceae		☺	
Phaseolus vulgaris	garden bean	Fabaceae		☺	
Physalis philadelphica	tomatillo	Solanaceae		☺	
Pisum sativum	pea	Fabaceae		☺	
Pisum sativum var. *macrocarpon*	sugar snap pea	Fabaceae		☺	
Rosmarinus officinalis	rosemary	Lamiaceae			
Rumex acetosa	common sorrel	Polygonaceae			
Rumex sanguineus	blood sorrel	Polygonaceae			◐
Rumex scutatus	French sorrel	Polygonaceae			◐
Satureja hortensis	summer savory	Lamiaceae			
Solanum lycopersicum	tomato	Solanaceae		☺	
Tagetes tenuifolia	signet marigold	Asteraceae		☺	
Tropaeolum majus	nasturtium	Tropaeolaceae		☺	◐
Viola species	pansy, Johnny jump-up, sweet violet	Violaceae			◐
Zea mays	corn	Poaceae		☺	

HERBACEOUS PERENNIALS

Agastache foeniculum	giant blue hyssop	Lamiaceae	N	☺	
Allium cepa × *proliferum*	walking onion	Alliaceae			◐
Allium cernuum	nodding onion	Alliaceae	N		
Allium schoenoprasum	chives	Alliaceae		☺	
Allium tricoccum	wild leek, ramp	Alliaceae	N		◐
Allium tuberosum	garlic chives, Chinese chives	Alliaceae			
Artemisia dracunculus	French tarragon	Asteraceae			
Asarum canadense	wild ginger	Aristolochiaceae	N		◐
Asparagus officinalis	asparagus	Asparagaceae			
Cynara cardunculus	cardoon	Asteraceae			
Cynara cardunculus (Scolymus group)	globe artichoke	Asteraceae			
Elymus virginicus	wild rye	Poaceae	N		
Foeniculum vulgare	fennel	Apiaceae			
Fragaria × *ananassa*	garden strawberry	Rosaceae		☺	◐

Species	Common name	Family	N	☺	◐
Fragaria vesca	woodland, alpine strawberry	Rosaceae			◐
Fragaria virginiana	wild strawberry	Rosaceae	N		◐
Galium odoratum	sweet woodruff	Rubiaceae			◐
Gaultheria procumbens	wintergreen	Ericaceae	N		◐
Helianthus tuberosus	Jerusalem artichoke	Asteraceae	N		
Lavendula species	lavender	Lamiaceae		☺	
Matteuccia struthiopteris	fiddleheads, ostrich fern	Onocleaceae	N		◐
Melissa officinalis	lemon balm	Lamiaceae		☺	◐
Mentha × piperita	peppermint	Lamiaceae		☺	◐
Mentha spicata	spearmint	Lamiaceae		☺	◐
Monarda didyma	scarlet bee balm	Lamiaceae	N		
Monarda fistulosa	wild bergamot, bee balm	Lamiaceae	N		
Origanum vulgare	oregano	Lamiaceae			
Rheum rhabarbarum	rhubarb	Polygonaceae			◐
Salvia officinalis	sage	Lamiaceae			
Satureja montana	winter savory	Lamiaceae			
Thymus serpyllum	creeping thyme	Lamiaceae			
Thymus vulgaris	thyme	Lamiaceae			

SHRUBS

Species	Common name	Family	N	☺	◐
Gaylussacia baccata	black huckleberry	Ericaceae	N		
Rubus fruticosus	blackberry	Rosaceae	N	☺	◐
Rubus idaeus	raspberry	Rosaceae	N	☺	◐
Rubus rolfei	creeping raspberry	Rosaceae			◐
Vaccinium angustifolium	lowbush blueberry	Ericaceae	N	☺	
Vaccinium corymbosum	highbush blueberry	Ericaceae	N	☺	◐

TREES

Species	Common name	Family	N	☺	◐
Amelanchier laevis	shadbush, Allegheny serviceberry	Rosaceae	N		◐
Asimina triloba	pawpaw	Annonaceae	N		
Carya ovata	shagbark hickory	Juglandaceae	N		
Diospyros virginiana	American persimmon	Ebenaceae	N		
Ficus carica	fig	Moraceae			
Juniperus communis	juniper	Cupressaceae	N		
Malus domestica	apple	Rosaceae		☺	
Prunus avium	sweet cherry	Rosaceae			
Prunus domestica	plum	Rosaceae			
Prunus persica	peach	Rosaceae			
Pyrus communis	pear	Rosaceae			

VINES

Species	Common name	Family	N	☺	◐
Actinidia arguta	hardy kiwi	Actinidiaceae		☺	
Passiflora incarnata	passion flower, maypop	Passifloraceae	N		
Vitis labrusca	fox grape	Vitaceae	N		◐
Vitis rotundifolia	muscadine grape	Vitaceae	N		
Vitis vinifera	wine grape	Vitaceae			

Planning Your Edible Garden

What are your goals? How would you like to enjoy your garden? Successful gardening begins with careful planning. Though you may be tempted to order all of the interesting new fruits and vegetables you've learned about in this book, you'll grow much better quality food if you first do a little homework and start with a plan.

Assess your site.

- Note the existing plants on your site. Some may need to be transplanted or removed. Others may cast shade or have unusual cultural requirements.
- Measure your site, and take note of any obstacles above or below ground, like electrical wires or pipes, as well as walls or paving that may create microclimates.
- Chart how much sun your garden gets, keeping in mind that edible plants generally require "full sun," which is at least six hours of direct sunlight.
- Know your area's hardiness zone (see www.arborday.org/media/zones.cfm).

Check your soil.

- Have your soil tested for contaminants and learn its pH and component nutrients.
- Determine your soil structure—is it clayey, loamy, or sandy? Loose or compacted? For a helpful drainage test, see page 19.
- Amend your soil as appropriate for the plants you have selected. Or plan to bring in new soil for raised beds or containers.

Plan for watering.

- Most food plants are thirsty plants. Research your area's average rainfall, then decide what sort of supplemental watering you will need.
- Slow, ground-level watering is best for most plants, so you may choose to install drip irrigation or soaker hoses.

Research plant choices.

- Consult seed and nursery catalogs to find fun and interesting plants with growing requirements that match your site conditions.
- Local nurseries and master gardener programs may offer lists of the cultivars that grow best in your region.

Time your harvests.

- Take note of days to maturity for each cultivar that you select, then make a calendar for starting your plants to provide a staggered harvest.
- Plant cool-season and warm-season edibles in succession to keep your beds occupied.

Protect your crops from weather and pests.

- Keep a vigilant eye out for harmful pests. Your local Cooperative Extension office can tell you the top pests to watch for in your area and provide management strategies.

For More Information

LOCAL RESOURCES

USDA Cooperative Extension System
www.csrees.usda.gov/Extension/
Local Cooperative Extensions provide essential services like soil testing, advice on pest control, and lists of cultivars that grow best in local conditions. Bear in mind, however, that their main constituency is farmers, so information is pitched toward agriculture. Some extensions offer home gardening sites, including the following:

Cornell Cooperative Extension
www.gardening.cornell.edu

Purdue Cooperative Extension
www.extension.purdue.edu/gardentips/
fruits.html

Rutgers Cooperative Extension
njaes.rutgers.edu/garden/

University of California Cooperative Extension's Common Ground Garden Program
celosangeles.ucdavis.edu/
Common_Ground_Garden_Program/

Master Gardener Programs
www.ahs.org/master_gardeners/
Master gardeners assist Cooperative Extension offices with garden education, demonstrations, school and community gardening, phone diagnostic service, research, and many other projects.

National Sustainable Agriculture Information Service (ATTRA)
attra.ncat.org
ATTRA, funded by the USDA, provides information and technical assistance to farmers, Cooperative Extension agents, educators, and others involved in sustainable agriculture. Online resources include planting guides, pest information, and links to regional organizations.

PLANT DATABASES
These online resources offer plant profiles and ethnobotanical information.

Mansfeld's World Database of Agricultural and Horticultural Crops
mansfeld.ipk-gatersleben.de/Mansfeld/

Plants for a Future
pfaf.org

Plant Resources of Southeast Asia
proseanet.org/prosea/

Plant Resources of Tropical Africa
www.prota.org

SEED COMPANIES AND NURSERIES
Many companies offer visual catalogs, background information, and horticultural tips; here are some of our favorites:

Baker Creek Heirloom Seeds
rareseeds.com

John Scheepers Kitchen Garden Seeds
kitchengardenseeds.com

Johnny's Selected Seeds
www.johnnyseeds.com+

Miller Nurseries
millernurseries.com

Raintree Nursery
www.raintreenursery.com

Seeds of Change
seedsofchange.com

St. Lawrence Nurseries
www.sln.potsdam.ny.us

Stark Bro's Nurseries & Orchards Co.
www.starkbros.com

Trade Winds Fruit
tradewindsfruit.com

SEED SAVING

These organizations support collecting and sharing heirloom seeds and plants.

Saving Our Seeds
savingourseeds.org

Seed Savers Exchange
seedsavers.org

BBG HANDBOOKS

Check out these other helpful guides published by Brooklyn Botanic Garden, available at bbg.org/handbooks.

Culture and Care

Healthy Soils for Sustainable Gardens

Natural Disease Control: A Common-Sense Approach to Plant First Aid

Natural Insect Control: The Ecological Gardener's Guide to Foiling Pests

Starting from Seed: The Natural Gardener's Guide to Propagating Plants

Plant Guides

The Best Apples to Buy and Grow

Buried Treasures: Tasty Tubers of the World

Chile Peppers: Hot Tips and Tasty Picks for Gardeners and Gourmets

Designing an Herb Garden

Gourmet Vegetables: Smart Tips and Tasty Picks

Growing Fruits: Nature's Desserts

Tantalizing Tomatoes: Smart Tips and Tasty Picks

Gardening Practice

Community Gardening

Essential Tools: Equipment and Supplies for Home Gardeners

Gardening With Children

BOOKS

The Art of French Vegetable Gardening
Louisa Jones, Artisan/Workman, 1995

The Backyard Orchardist
Stella Otto, Ottographics, 1995

Creative Vegetable Gardening
Joy Larkcom, MITCH, 2008

Edible Landscaping
Rosalind Creasy, Sierra Club, 2010

Food Plants of the World:
An Illustrated Guide
Ben-Erik van Wyk, Timber Press, 2005

Fruits and Berries for the
Home Garden
Lewis Hill, Storey Publishing, 1992

The Garden Primer
Barbara Damrosch, Workman Publishing, 2008

Grow Great Grub: Organic Food
from Small Spaces
Gayla Trail, Clarkson Potter, 2010

Growing Fruit (RHS Encyclopedia
of Practical Gardening)
Harry Baker, Mitchell Beazley, 1999

Landscaping with Fruit
Lee Reich, Storey Publishing, 2009

The New Oxford Book of Food Plants
J.G. Vaughan and C.A. Geissler, Oxford University Press USA, 2009

Vegetables
Roger Phillips and Martyn Rix, Macmillan, 2007

BLOGS

Garden Rant
www.gardenrant.com

You Grow Girl
www.yougrowgirl.com

Contributors

Joni Blackburn is the copyeditor at Brooklyn Botanic Garden. In addition to copy-editing BBG's handbooks for nearly ten years, she has contributed articles about horticulture to *Plants & Gardens News* and other publications. She grows vegetables, blackberries, raspberries, currents, and ornamental plants at her family's farmhouse in the Catskills.

Barbara Damrosch writes a weekly column for the *Washington Post* called "A Cook's Garden" and is the author of *Theme Gardens* and the classic guide *The Garden Primer*. She has appeared as a correspondent on the PBS series *The Victory Garden* and cohosted *Gardening Naturally* on TLC. She practiced landscape design from 1978 to 1992 and now grows vegetables and flowers commercially in Maine at Four Season Farm with her husband, Eliot Coleman.

Ashley Gamell cares for Brooklyn Botanic Garden's Discovery Garden and Education Greenhouse and coordinates nature-based Discovery programs for families. Previously, she coordinated BBG's Children's Garden, where kids have been growing food for nearly 100 years. Gamell earned a degree in environmental studies and writing from Middlebury College and is also a plant-inspired poet.

Caleb Leech is curator of the Herb Garden and Hardy Fern Collection at Brooklyn Botanic Garden and former curator of BBG's Alice Recknagel Ireys Fragrance Garden. He spent his early childhood on New England farms. By his 20s, he was working in his family's Cape Cod landscape business and finding time to volunteer at the local CSA. Leech has also worked for seed foundations, permaculture gardens, and a hospital healing garden.

Cayleb Long is curator of the Annual and Perennial Borders, Lily Pools, and Magnolia Plaza at Brooklyn Botanic Garden, where he has worked since 2006. A native Oregonian, Long has developed gardens in New York, Oregon, Michigan, and Florida. He teaches plant identification and soil science courses for BBG's Horticulture Certificate program and pursues interests in organic gardening, sustainable ecologies, and the local food movement.

Ulrich Lorimer is curator of the Native Flora Garden at Brooklyn Botanic Garden and holds a degree in landscape horticulture from the University of Delaware. He teaches classes in gardening, native plants, integrated pest management, and botany at BBG and New York Botanical Garden. He has contributed to the BBG books *Healthy Soils for Sustainable Gardens*, *Community Gardening*, and *Great Natives for Tough Places*.

Joan McDonald is a former manager of the Gardener's Resource Center at Brooklyn Botanic Garden. She runs Gardens by Joan (gardensbyjoan.com), a Brooklyn-based garden design business. She is a regular contributor to BBG's *Plants & Gardens News*, wrote a chaper for the BBG book *Great Natives for Tough Places*, and teaches classes on garden design and sustainable gardening at BBG.

Elizabeth Peters is the director of Publications at Brooklyn Botanic Garden, where she publishes the Guides for a Greener Planet imprint and oversees the Garden's website, bbg.org. She edited the BBG books *Community Gardening* and *The Tree Book for Kids and Their Grown-ups*. From 1990 to 1992 Peters coordinated Tuscarora Organic Growers, a collective of small central Pennsylvania family farms.

Meghan Ray worked at Brooklyn Botanic Garden from 1994 until 2006 as curator of the Shakespeare Garden, Alice Recknagel Ireys Fragrance Garden, and the Rock Garden, among others. She now manages the South African and palm and cycad collections at the University of California Botanical Garden at Berkeley. Ray has a master's degree in garden history and landscape studies from Bard Graduate Center and writes and teaches about horticulture and landscape history.

Jennifer Williams has worked as a gardener in Brooklyn Botanic Garden's Steinhardt Conservatory for more than ten years, specializing in interior plant display and container design. She also cares for the Woodland Garden and designs BBG's annual holiday exhibit. Williams is a graduate of the University of Georgia, where she studied drawing and painting.

ILLUSTRATIONS
Elizabeth Ennis

PHOTOS
Catherine Anstet pages 30, 102

Laura Berman cover, pages 4, 13, 15, 26, 34, 54, 55 [2], 57 [3], 61 [1, 2], 65 [2, 3, 4, 6], 71, 72, 73 [1, 2], 76, 77 [1, 3, 4, 5, 6], 80 [2, 5], 81 [3], 82, 85 [3, 4, 5], 86 [3], 89 [2], 94, 97 [1, 3], 98, 100 [6], 101 [6], 103 [5], 104 [2, 3], 107 [2, 3, 4]

Rebecca Bullene pages 7, 42, 69 [2, 3], 73 [4], 77 [2], 104 [5], 107 [1]

David Cavagnaro pages 16, 50, 55 [3, 4, 5], 56, 57 [2], 65 [1], 67 [2], 73 [3, 6], 80 [1, 4, 6], 81 [4, 5], 85 [1, 2, 6], 86 [2, 5, 6], 91 [2], 93 [1], 100 [4, 5], 101 [2, 4], 103 [3], 107 [5]

Barbara Damrosch pages 2, 8, 11, 12, 22, 63, 79, 89 [1, 3]

Sonnia Hill page 95 [1]

Bill Johnson pages 57 [1], 59 [2], 65 [5], 67 [1], 69 [1], 86 [1, 4], 93 [2], 100 [1, 2], 101 [1], 104 [1, 4]

Ulrich Lorimer pages 60, 103 [6]

Chris Kreussling pages 75, 95 [2]

Jerry Pavia pages 18, 55 [1, 6], 81 [1, 2], 83, 90, 100 [3], 101 [3, 5], 103 [1, 2, 4], 107 [6]

Antonio Rosario page 46

Clara Sardin page 80 [3]

Gayla Trail pages 59 [1], 64, 73 [5], 91 [1, 3], 97 [2], 104 [6]

Index

Note: Page references in italics refer to illustrations or captions.

A

Abelmoschus esculentus, 24, *104*, 105, 108
  'Aunt Hetties Red', 39
  'Little Lucy', 23, 25
  'Red Burgundy', 13
Actinidia arguta, 15, *15*, 19–21, 94, 110
Agastache foeniculum, 28–29, 87, 109
  'Blue Fortune', 14
Allegheny serviceberry (*Amelanchier laevis*), 27, *29*, 76, *76*, 110
Allium species, 52
  ampeloprasum var. *ampeloprasum*, 55, *55*, 108
  ampeloprasum var. *porrum*, 16–17, *37*, 53–54, 55, *55*, 108
    'Bleu of Solaise', 37
  cepa, 27, 52–53, 108
    'French Red', 37
    'Yellow Granex', 39
  cepa var. *aggregatum*, 54, 55, 108
  cepa × *proliferum*, *40*, 55, *55*, 109
  cernuum, 55, *55*, 109
  fistulosum, 108
    'Santa Claus', 54
  ramosum, 55
  sativum, 53, 108
  schoenoprasum, 14, *21*, 36, 53, 109
    'Forescate', 54
  triccocum, 27, *29*, 54, *54*, 109
  tuberosum, 38–39, 51, 55, *55*, 109
Amaranthus tricolor, 43, *45*, 56, *56*, 108
Amelanchier laevis, 27, *29*, 76, *76*, 110
Ananas comosus, 108
Anethum graveolens, 80, *80*, 108
  'Bouquet', *39*, 80
  'Fernleaf', 80
Anthriscus cerefolium, 78–79, *80*, 108
  'Great Green', 37
Apple (*Malus domestica*), 14, *33*, 75–76, 110
Artemisia dracunculus, 108
  'Sativa', 37
Artichokes, 13
  globe (*Cynara cardunculus* (Scolymus group)), 66–67, *67*, 109
  Jerusalem (*Helianthus tuberosus*), 28–29, 104–105, 110
Asarum canadense, 28–29, 109

Asimina triloba, 15, 27, *29*, 106, 110
Asparagus (*Asparagus officinalis*), 14, 19, *21*, *79*, 103, *103*, 109

B

Basella alba, *104*, 105, 108
  'Rubra', 105
Basil (*Ocimum basilicum*), 36, *41*, *49*, 85, 109
  cinnamon, 38
  French, 37
  globe, *25*, 85
  Thai, 43, *45*, 85
Beans
  garden/pole (*Phaseolus vulgaris*), *25*, *49*, 90–91, *90–91*, 109
  scarlet runner (*Phaseolus coccineus*), 90, *90*, 109
Bee balm (*Monarda fistulosa*), 28–29, *86*, 87, 110
Beets (*Beta vulgaris*), 13, 23, *25*, *41*, 48–49, 56–57, 108
Bergamot, wild (*Monarda fistulosa*), 28–29, *86*, 87, 110
Beta vulgaris, 56
  'Bull's Blood', 13, 23, *25*, *41*, 57
  'Chioggia', 48–49, 57
  var. *cicla*, *4–5*, 12, 108
    'Bright Lights', 48–49, 57
    'Golden Sunrise', 57
    'Ruby Red', 57
Blackberries (*Rubus fruticosus*), 58–59, *59*, 110
Blueberries
  highbush (*Vaccinium corymbosum*), 19, *21*, 27, *29*, *33*, 60–61, *61*, 110
  lowbush (*Vaccinium angustifolium*), 19, 27, *29*, 60–61, *61*, 110
Borage (*Borago officinalis*), 57, 99, *100*, *102*, 108
Brambles. See blackberries; raspberries
Brassica species, 62–63
  juncea, 64, 108
    'Osaka Purple', *41*, 64
    'Red Giant', *41*, 64
    'Southern Giant Curled', *39*, 64
  oleracea, 12
    'Lacinato', *8–9*, *25*, *41*, *45*, *49*, 51, 63, 65, *65*
    var. *acephala*, *50–51*, 65, 108
    var. *botrytis*, 62–64, 108
      'Veronica', *25*, 64
    var. *capitata*, *65*, 108
      'Copenhagen Market', 64
      'Mammoth Red', 64
      'Tendersweet', 64

Gemmifera group, 64, 108
  'Long Island', 65
  'Red Bull', 65
  var. *gongylodes*, 62, *65*, 108
    'Kolibri', 65
    'Superschmelz', 65
  var. *italica*, 13–14, 62, 108
    'De Cicco', 63
    'Green Comet', 63
  var. *sabellica*, 105, 108
    'Osaka Red', *2*
Broccoli (*Brassica oleracea* var. *italica*), 13–14, 62–63, 108
Brooklyn Botanic Garden, 6, 7, 44, 46, *46*
Brussels sprouts (*Brassica oleracea*, Gemmifera group), 64, 108
Bulb fennel (*Foeniculum vulgare* subsp. *vulgare*, Azoricum group), *25*, 80, 109

C

Cabbages (*Brassica oleracea* var. *capitata*), 64, *65*, 108
Calendula (*Calendula officinalis*), 99, *99*
Capsicum species
  annuum
    'Ancho 101', *38*, 69, 108
    'Black Pearl', *41*, 69, *69*
    'Holy Mole', 69
    'Hungarian Yellow Wax', 69
    'Purple Jalapeño', *38*, 108
  chinense, 108
    'Chocolate Habanero', *38*, 69
Cardomom (*Elettaria cardamomum*), 36, *40*, 109
Cardoons (*Cynara cardunculus*), 23, *25*, 43, *45*, 66–67, *67*, 109
Carnation (*Dianthus caryophyllus*), *21*, 99–100, 109
Carrots (*Daucus carota* subsp. *sativus* var. *sativus*), 5, *25*, *49*, 82, *82*, 109
Carya ovata, 27, *29*, 110
Cauliflower (*Brassica oleracea* var. *botrytis*), 12, 62–64, 108
Celosia argentea, 43, *45*, 110
Chard (*Beta vulgaris* var. *cicla*), *4–5*, 12, 48–49, 56–57, 108
Cherries
  sour (*Prunus cerasus*), 77, *77*
  sweet (*Prunus avium*), *33*, 77, *77*, 110
Cherry tomato (*Solanum lycopersicum* var. *cerasiforme*), *49*, 97, *97*, 109
Chervil (*Anthriscus cerefolium*), 37, 78–79, *80*, 108

Children's Garden (Brooklyn Botanic Garden), 6, 46, *46*

Chile peppers. See peppers

Chives (*Allium schoenoprasum*), 14, *21, 36, 53*, 54, *55*, 109

Chives, Chinese (*Allium tuberosum*), 38–39, 51, 55, *55*, 109

Cilantro (*Coriandrum sativum*), *25, 36, 38*, 79, *80*, 108

Citrullus lanatus, 71, 73, *73*, 108
  'Cream of Saskatchewan', 73
  'Golden Midget', 73
  'Moon and Stars', 23, *25*, 73, *73*

Clove pink (*Dianthus caryophyllus*), *21*, 99–100, 109

Cockscomb (*Celosia argentea*), 43, *45*, 110

Collards (*Brassica oleracea* var. *acephala*), *50–51*, 65, 108

Compost, 19–20, 36

Container gardening, 32, *34*, 35–41, *37–41*

Coriander (*Coriandrum sativum*), 36, 79, *80*, 108
  'Calypso', *25*, 79
  'Slo-Bolt', 38

Corn (*Zea mays*), 5, 14, *16–17, 25, 103*, 109

Cottage gardens, 19

Crabapples, 14–15

Creasy, Rosalind: *Edible Landscaping*, 15

Creeping thyme (*Thymus serpyllum*), *25*, 86, 110

Crithmum maritimum, 43, *45*, 81, *81*, 108

Cucumber (*Cucumis sativus*), *39*, 72–73, *73*

Cucumis species
  melo, 73, *73*, 108
    'Golden Beauty', 73
    'Minnesota Midget', 73
  sativus, *73*, 108
    'Crystal Apple', 72–73
    'Homemade Pickles', 39
    'Parisian Pickling', 73

Cucurbita species, 70–72
  maxima, 72, 109
    'Marina di Chioggia', 72
  moschata, 72, 109
  pepo, *8–9*, 72, *73*, 109
    'Baby Boo', 72
    'Black Beauty', 71
    'Cocozelle', *25*, 71
    'Eight Ball', 71
    'Gill's Golden Pippin', 72
    'Pattison Panache Verte et Blanc', 71
    'Spacemiser', 49
    'Summer Crookneck', 71
    'Yellow Crookneck', 25

Cumin (*Cuminum cyminum*), *38, 38*, 79–80, *80*, 109

Cynara
  cardunculus, 23, *25*, 43, *45*, 66, *67*
    'Gobbo di Nizza', 67
    'Porto Spineless', 67
    Scolymus group, 66, 67, *67*, 109
      'Green Globe', 67
      'Imperial Star', 67
      'Violetto', 67

D

Daucus carota subsp. *sativus* var. *sativus*, 5, 82, *82*, 109
  'Bolero'', 82
  'Purple Haze', *25*, 82
  'Rainbow', 49
  'Red Samurai', *25*, 82
  'White Kuttinger', 82
  'Yellowstone', *25*, 82

Dianthus (*Dianthus caryophyllus*), *21*, 99, 109
  'Enfant de Nice', 100
  'Fenbow Nutmeg Clove', 100

Dill (*Anethum graveolens*), *39*, 80, *80*, 108

Diospyros virginiana, 15, 27, *29*, 106, 110

Drainage, 19, 36

E

Edible plants, overview of, 5–7, *7*, 8–15

Eggplant, 13

Elettaria cardamomum, 36, *40*, 109

Elymus virginicus, 28, *29*, 110

F

Fennel (*Foeniculum vulgare*), 23, *25*, *41*, 78, 80, *79–80*, 109

Ficus carica, 19, *21, 103*, 104, 110
  'Brown Turkey', *33*, 104

Fiddleheads (ostrich fern; *Matteuccia struthiopteris*), 27–29, *40, 103*, 104, 110

Fig (*Ficus carica*), 19, *21, 33, 103*, 104, 110

Foeniculum vulgare, 23, 78, 80, *80, 81*
  'Purpureum', 80
  'Smokey', 41
  subsp. *vulgare* Azoricum group, *79*, 80, 109
  'Zefa Fino', *25*, 80

Fox grape (*Vitis labrusca*), *29*, 95, 110

Fragaria species, 92–93
  × ananassa, *21*, 92–93, *93*, 110
    'Frel', 93
    'Honeoye', *33*
    'Ozark Beauty', *39*, 93
    'Seascape', 93
    'Tribute', *33*
    'Variegata', 93

  vesca, 14, 43, *45*, 92–93, 110
    'Lipstick', 93
    'Rügen', 93
  semperflorens 'Yellow Wonder', 93
  virginiana, 28–29, 92–93, *93*, 110
    'Little Scarlet', 93

French tarragon (*Artemisia dracunculus*), *37*, 108

G

Galium odoratum, 101, 102, 110

Garlic (*Allium sativum*), 53, 55, 108

Garlic, elephant (*Allium ampeloprasum* var. *ampeloprasum*), 55, 108

Garlic chives (*Allium tuberosum*), 38–39, 51, 55, *55*, 109

Gaultheria procumbens, 28, *29*, 107, *107*, 110

Gaylussacia baccata, 27, *29*, 60, *60*, 110

Geraniums, scented (*Pelargonium* species), 100, *100*, 109

Ginger (*Asarum canadense*), 28–29, 109

Grapes, 15, 94
  fox (*Vitis labrusca*), 28–29, 95, 110
  muscadine (*Vitis rotundifolia*), 94–95, *95*
  wine (*Vitis vinifera*), *33*, 95, *95*, 110

H

Helianthus species
  annuus, *101*, 102, 105, 109
    'Mammoth Grey Stripe', 49
    'Mongolian Giant', 102
  tuberosus, 28, *29*, 104, 110
    'Red Fuseau', 105

Herb Garden (Brooklyn Botanic Garden), 6, 44

Heritage Farm (Decorah, Iowa), 14

Hickory, shagbark (*Carya ovata*), 27, *29*, 110

Huckleberry (*Gaylussacia baccata*), 27, *29*, 60, *60*, 110

Hyssop (*Agastache foeniculum*), 14, 28, *29*, 86, 87, 109

I

Impatiens (*Impatiens walleriana*), 99, 100, *100*, 109

Interplanting, 10

Ipomoea batatas, 109
  'Blackie', 41
  'Vardaman', 39

J

Johnny jump-ups (*Viola tricolor*), 101, *101*, 109

Joseph's coat (*Amaranthus tricolor*), 43, *45*, 56, *56*, 108

Juniper (*Juniperus communis*), 19, *21,* 110

K

Kale (*Brassica oleracea* var. *sabellica*), 2, 8–9, 13, *50–51,* 65, 108
Kiwi (*Actinidia arguta*), 15, *15,* 19–21, 94, 110
Kohlrabi (*Brassica oleracea* var. *gongylodes*), 62, 65, *65,* 108

L

Lactuca sativa, 5–6, 12, *50–51,* 88–89, *89,* 109
  'Black Seeded Simpson', 47, 49
  'Brune d'Hiver', *37,* 89
  'Forellenschluss', 89
  'Gotte Jaune d'Or', *37,* 89
  'Lollo Rosso Dark', *37,* 89
  'Red Velvet', 89
  'Rouge Grenobloise', *37,* 89
  'Vulcan', 89
  'Web's Wonderful', 89
  'Yugoslavian Red Butterhead', 89
Landscaping with Fruits (Reich), 15
Lavender (*Lavendula* species), 51, 54, 86, *86,* 110
  English (*L. angustifolia*), 86
  × *intermedia* 'Hidcote Giant', 87
  'Munstead', 86–87
  'Rosea', 86
Leeks (*Allium* species)
  ampeloprasum var. *porrum,* 16–17, *37,* 53–54, 55, 108
  triccocum (wild leek), 27, *29,* 52, 54, *54,* 109
Lemon balm (*Melissa officinalis*), *40,* 84–85, *85,* 110
Lettuce (*Lactuca sativa*), 5–6, 12, *37,* 47, *49, 50–51,* 88–89, *89,* 109
Levisticum officinale, 19, *21,* 78, 80–81, *81,* 109
Lovage (*Levisticum officinale*), 19, *21,* 78, 80–81, *81,* 109

M

Maize. See corn
Malus domestica, 14, 75–76, *77,* 110
  'Golden Sentinel', *33,* 75–76
  'Northpole', *33*
Marigolds (*Tagetes tenuifolia*), 13, 14, 44–45, 98, *98,* 100–101, *101,* 109. *See also* calendula
Matteuccia struthiopteris, 27–29, *40, 103,* 104, 110
Maypop (*Passiflora incarnata*), *33, 104,* 105, 110
Melissa officinalis, 40, 84–85, *85,* 110
Melons, *71,* 73, 108
  bitter (*Momordica charantia*), 72, *72,* 109
  cantaloupe, 73
  casaba, 73

honeydew, 73
muskmelon, 73, *73*
watermelon, 23, *25,* 73, *73,* 108
Mentha
  × *piperita, 40, 53,* 84, *85,* 110
    'Chocolate Mint', 84
    'Lime Mint', 84
    'Orange Mint', 84
    'Variegata', 84
  spicata, 25, 40, 84, *85,* 110
    'Kentucky Colonel', 84
Momordica charantia, 72, *72,* 109
Monarda
  didyma, 87, 110
  fistulosa, 28–29, *86,* 87, 110
Mulching, 24, 48
Muscadine (*Vitis rotundifolia*), 94–95, *95*
Mustard greens (*Brassica juncea*), *39, 41,* 64, *64,* 108

N

Nasturtiums (*Tropaeolum majus*), 43–44, 48–49, 99, 101, *101,* 109

O

Ocimum basilicum, 36, 85, 109
  'Genovese", 49
  'Marseillais", 37
  'Mexican Spice", 38
  'Pistou', *25,* 85
  'Red Rubin", 41
  'Siam Queen", 43, *45,* 85, *85*
Okra (*Abelmoschus esculentus*), 13, 23–25, *39, 104,* 105, 108
Onions
  Allium cepa, 27, 52–53, 108
    Vidalia, *39,* 52
  bunching (*Allium fistulosum*), 54, 108
  nodding (*Allium cernuum*), 55, 109
  walking (*Allium cepa × proliferum*), *40,* 55, *55,* 109
Orchards, *30,* 30–33, *33*
Oregano (*Origanum vulgare*), 85, *85*
  'Aureum', 44–45, *53*
  Greek (subsp. *hirtum*), 85, 110
  'Zorba Red', 14
Organic matter, 9–10
Ostrich fern (*Matteuccia struthiopteris*), 27–29, *40,* 104, *104,* 110

P

Pansies (*Viola × wittrockiana*), 101, *101–102,* 109
Parsley (*Petroselinum crispum*), 14, *25,* 78, 81, *81,* 109
Passiflora incarnata, 15, *33, 104,* 105, 110
Passion flower (*Passiflora incarnata*), 15, *33, 104,* 105, 110

Pawpaw (*Asimina triloba*), 15, 27, *29, 104,* 106, 110
Peach (*Prunus persica*), 14, *33,* 75, 76, *77,* 110
Pear (*Pyrus communis*), *33,* 76–77, *77,* 110
Peas (*Pisum sativum*), *25, 104,* 106, 109
Pelargonium species, 100, *100,* 109
Peppermint (*Mentha × piperita*), *40, 53,* 84, 110
Peppers, 68–69
  ancho, *38,* 108
  bell, 69
  cayenne, 69, *69*
  datil, 69
  habanero, *38,* 69, *69,* 108
  Hungarian, 69
  Jalapeño, *38,* 69, 108
  poblano, 69, 108
  Scotch bonnet, 69, 108
  serrano, 69, 108
Persimmon (*Diospyros virginiana*), 15, 27, *29,* 106, 110
Petroselinum crispum, 14, 78, 81, *81,* 109
  'Grüne Perle', 81
  'Italian Flat Leaf', 25
  var. *neopolitanum,* 81
Phaseolus species
  coccineus, 90, *90,* 109
  vulgaris, 90, *90,* 109
    'Borlotto Solista', 91
    'Kentucky Wonder', *25,* 91
    'Marvel of Venice', *49,* 91
Physalis philadelphica, 107, *107,* 109
  'Toma Verde', 38
Pickle tubs, *39*
Pineapple (*Ananas comosus*), 108
Pisum sativum, 106, 109
  var. *macrocarpon, 25,* 106, 109
Plum (*Prunus domestica*), 14–15, 77, *77,* 110
Pollination, 20, 28, 31
Potagers, ornamental, 22, 22–25, *25*
Potatoes, 13
Prunus species
  avium, 77, 110
    'Stella', *33,* 77
  cerasus, 77
  domestica, 14–15, 77, *77,* 110
  persica, 14, *75,* 76, *77,* 110
    'Dwarf Elberta', *33*
  salicina, 77
Public gardens, *42,* 42–45, *45*
Pyrus communis, 76–77, *77,* 110
  'Moonglow', *33*
  'Seckel', *33*

R

Ramp (wild leek; *Allium triccocum*), 27, *29,* 52, 54, *54,* 109

Raspberries (*Rubus idaeus*), *33, 49,*
58–59, *59,* 110
Raspberries, creeping (*Rubus rolfei*),
19, *21,* 59, 110
Red shallot (*Allium cepa*), 37
Red tassel flower (*Emilia coccinea*), 24
Reich, Lee: *Landscaping with Fruits,*
15
Rheum rhabarbarum, 43, *45,* 106,
107, 110
'Crimson Red', 39
Rhubarb (*Rheum rhabarbarum*), *39,*
43, *45,* 106, *107,* 110
Rock samphire (*Crithmum
maritimum*), 43, *45,* 81, *81,*
108
Romanesco (*Brassica oleracea* var.
botrytis), *25,* 63, 65, 108
Rosemary (*Rosmarinus officinalis*),
83, 85, 109
'Prostratus', 85–86
Rubus
fruticosus, 58–59, *59,* 110
'Black Satin," 59
idaeus, *59,* 110
'Heritage', *33,* 49
'Kiwigold', 59
rolfei, 19, *21,* 59, 110
Rumex
acetosa, *21,* 107, 109
sanguineus, *37,* 107, *107,* 109
scutatus 'Silver Buckler', *37,* 43,
45, 107, 109
Rye (*Elymus virginicus*), 28, *29,* 110

S

Sage (*Salvia officinalis*), *13,* 14, *25,
41,* 51, *83,* 86, *86,* 110
Salvia officinalis, *13,* 14, *83,* 86,
86, 110
'Purpurescens', *41,* 51
'Tricolor', *25,* 51, 86
Satureja hortensis, 86, 87, 109
Satureja montana, 19, *21,* 87, 109
Savory
summer (*Satureja hortensis*), 86,
87, 109
winter (*Satureja montana*), 19, *21,*
87, 110
Scallions (*Allium fistulosum*), 54, 108
Scarlet bee balm (*Monarda didyma*),
87, 110
Seed Savers Exchange (Decorah,
Iowa), 14
Shadbush (*Amelanchier laevis*), 27,
29, 76, *76,* 110
Shallots (*Allium cepa* var.
aggregatum), 54, 55, 108
Signet marigolds. See marigolds
Soil
drainage, 19
testing, 9, 24

Solanum lycopersicum, 109
'Banana Legs', 97
'Brandywine', 23, *25,* 97
'Chadwick', *49,* 97
'Chocolate Cherry', *38,* 97
'Gold Nugget', 97
'Roma', 97
'Spears Tennessee Green', *39,* 97
'Striped Roman', 97
'Tiny Tim', 97
Sorrel
blood (*Rumex sanguineus*), *37,*
107, *107,* 109
common (*Rumex acetosa*), *21,*
107, 109
French (*Rumex scutatus*), *37,* 43,
45, 107, 109
Spearmint (*Mentha spicata*), *25,* 40,
84, *85,* 110
Spinach, Malabar (*Basella alba*), *104,*
105, 108
Squashes, *71*
summer (*Cucurbita pepo*), 8–9,
25, 49, 72, *73,* 109
winter (*Cucurbita* species), 8–9,
72, 109
Strawberries, *12,* 92–93, *93*
alpine (*Fragaria vesca*), 14, 43, *45,*
93, *93,* 110
beach (*Fragaria chiloensis*), 93
garden (*Fragaria × ananassa*), *21,*
33, 39, 93, *93,* 110
wild (*Fragaria virginiana*), 28–29,
93, *93,* 110
woodland (*Fragaria vesca*), 43, *45,*
93, 110
Succession planting, *7,* 10
Sugar snap peas (*Pisum sativum* var.
macrocarpon), *25,* 106, 109
Sunflower (*Helianthus annuus*), *49,*
102, 104–105, 109
Sweet potatoes (*Ipomoea batatas*), *39,*
41, 109

T

Tagetes tenuifolia, *13,* 44–45, 100–
101, *101,* 109
'Lemon Gem', 14
'Tangerine Gem', *98*
Thyme (*Thymus vulgaris*), 14, *37,*
86, *86,* 110
Thymus species
serpyllum, *25,* 86, 110
vulgaris, 86, *86,* 110
'Narrow Leaf French', 37
Tilling, 24
Tomatillos (*Physalis philadelphica*),
38, 107, *107,* 109
Tomatoes (*Solanum lycopersicum*),
23, 96
beefsteak, 97
cherry (var. *cerasiforme*), *49,* 97,
97, 109

globe, *49,* 97, *97*
plum, 97
Trees
fruit, 74–77, *75–77*
native food forest and meadow,
26–29
orchards, *30,* 30–33, *33*
Tropaeolum majus, 43–44, 99, *101,*
109
'Alaska', 101
'Jewel Mix', 48–49, 101
Tuscan Kale (*Brassica oleracea*
'Lacinato'), 8–9, 13, *25, 41, 45,*
49, 51, *63,* 65, *65*

V

Vaccinium
angustifolium, 19, 27, *29,* 60–61,
61, 110
'Top Hat', 61
corymbosum, 19, *21,* 27, *29,*
60–61, *61,* 110
'Bluecrop', *33,* 61
'Elliot', 61
'Herbert', *33*
'Jubilee', 61
'Patriot', 61
'Sharpblue', 61
Verbena (*Verbena bonariensis*), 24
Vertical gardening, *7,* 11
Viola species, *40,* 99
odorata, 101, *101,* 109
tricolor, 101, *101,* 109
× wittrockiana, 101, *101–102*
Violets (*Viola odorata*), 101, *101,* 109
Vitis, 15
labrusca, 28–29, 95, 110
'Concord', 95
rotundifolia, *94,* 95, *95*
'Carlos', 95
'Nesbitt', 95
vinifera, *95,* 95, 110
'Lakemont', *33,* 95
'Suffolk Red', *33,* 95
'Thompson Seedless', 95

W

Watermelon (*Citrullus lanatus*), 23,
25, 71, 73, *73,* 108
Wintergreen (*Gaultheria procumbens*),
28–29, 107, *107,* 110
Woodruff (*Galium odoratum*), *101,*
102, 110

Z

Zea mays, 5, 14, *16–17, 103,* 109
'Chires Baby', 103
'Painted Mountain', 49
'Stowell's Sweet', 25
Zucchini (*Cucurbita pepo*), *25, 49,*
71, *73*

PROVIDING EXPERT GARDENING ADVICE FOR OVER 65 YEARS

Join Brooklyn Botanic Garden as an annual Subscriber Member and have new gardening handbooks delivered directly to you, plus BBG newsletters, mailings, and privileges at many botanic gardens across the country. Visit bbg.org/subscribe for details.

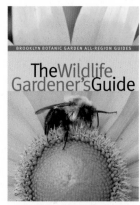

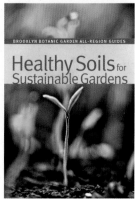

BBG GUIDES FOR A GREENER PLANET

World renowned for pioneering gardening information, Brooklyn Botanic Garden's award-winning guides provide practical advice in a compact format for gardeners across North America. To order other fine titles, shop online at bbg.org/handbooks or call 718-623-7280. To learn more about Brooklyn Botanic Garden,